Supreme Ultimate

Also by Patrick McDermott:

Workflow Modeling
Tools for Process Improvement and Application Development
(With Alec Sharp)

The Systems Analyst as Internal Consultant

Zen and the Art of Systems Analysis
Meditations on Computer Systems Development

Karate's Supreme Ultimate

The Taikyoku Kata
in
Five Rings

Patrick McDermott
&
Ferol Arce

iUniverse, Inc.
New York Lincoln Shanghai

Karate's Supreme Ultimate
The Taikyoku Kata in Five Rings

iUniverse, Inc.

For information address:
iUniverse, Inc.
2021 Pine Lake Road, Suite 100
Lincoln, NE 68512
www.iuniverse.com

ISBN: 0-595-30747-7

Printed in the United States of America

Himeyuri is the most beautiful heroine of Okinawan folk tales. Her name in English is Princess Lily. There is another beautiful princess, named Lilian.

To my Princess Lily

Duke always had a twinkle in his eyes, and always made you feel as though you were on the right track with whatever you were trying to accomplish.

Raymond Victor "Duke" Moore
Hanshi, Zen Budokai 10th Dan
(April 19, 1915-February 25, 2003)

Contents

Illustrations & Tables

Technique

In your effort for technique
With the hands and feet
There is something to keep
A feeling that is deep.
It is the fighting spirit
You can almost hear it
Whispering
"To make it, I have to care
To do it I have to be there
To block or strike takes time and space
To train sincerely is to keep the pace."

After the sweat of the day
Just go to a mirror and look at yourself
And see what that person has to say.
Know that the transition of learning
The belts that you are earning
And the test of fail or pass.
The person whose verdict counts most in your life
Is the one staring back from the glass.

Just as the bow is to the cord
The shield is to the sword
Just as the block is to the punch
The teacher was a student once.
The bow and the cord help the arrow go
The student and the teacher help each other grow.
The darkness of the sky makes the stars bright,
Complementing each other in the night.
Karate Dō is learning much more than how to fight.

JOHN PEREIRA

Acknowledgements

The Japanese writing in the book was produced with Stephen Chung's JWP Japanese Word Processor, distributed under the GNU General Public License, available from The Monash Nihongo ftp Archive at Monash University, Melbourne, Australia http://ftp.monash.edu.au/pub/nihongo/. The archive is maintained by Jim Breen (jwb@csse.monash.edu.au) as part of an invaluable repository of files and software related to Japan, its people, and particularly the Japanese language. Thanks to Stephen, Jim and all the many contributors to the Japanese Dictionary and software available there.

❧ ❧ ❧

Miyamoto Musashi at the age of 13 killed his first opponent in a sword fight, Arima Kihei. At 16 he killed Akiyama from Tajima Province (today's Hyogo, where Kobe is located). In his most famous encounter, he fought and killed Sasaki Kojiro with an oar. The ancient Egyptians believed your fortunes in the afterworld would improve every time your name was spoken by the living. In that spirit we try to mention names whenever possible. Since brave men died, we mention the names of the losers of these encounters. In a sense, they died that this book might be produced. Please maintain a similar spirit of respect for your opponents.

❧ ❧ ❧

Patrick would like to thank his second Sensei, Grant Butterfield of the Bladium Sports Club in Alameda, California. He always seems to have an encouraging word just when it's needed. Thanks to all the Sempai who have helped along the Way, and served as inspiration, especially: Vasundara Barron, Jody Linick, Michael Pollard, and Don Stasenka.

An event that set Patrick on this path of learning about martial arts was a chance attendance at a Samurai Game ®. The Game was invented by writer and teacher George Leonard, author of a number of books, including *Mastery, Education & Ecstasy, The Ultimate Athlete*, and *The Silent Pulse*, and was sponsored as an extracurricular activity by his second (Master's Degree) alma mater, the University of San Francisco. The session was conducted by Lance Giroux, the President of Allied Ronin Leadership Training & Consulting™ (www.AlliedRonin.com). Patrick says: "Although it is just a game, and I usually find games a waste of time, this game is almost spiritual. In any event, it started me thinking on Things Japanese and Things Martial Arts, and eventually I decided to study Karate."

☯ ☯ ☯

Thanks to Lilian Roberts and Jody Linick for reviewing the manuscript, and helping with the logistics, proofreading and indexing.

☯ ☯ ☯

To Lilian Roberts and all the other Karate widows and widowers, thanks for your support, understanding, and encouragement.

The Obligatory Orthographic Notes

The order of names in Japanese and Chinese is the opposite of English, with the family name first, and the given name last (don't you dare say the last name comes first!). We generally show names in Western order, given name first, family name last, except when historic usage dictates otherwise.

❧ ❧ ❧

The names of waza, kata, ryu and martial arts are treated as proper nouns, and so capitalized. Since Japanese doesn't have an equivalent of capitalization, and words are never spaced out in a sentence, spacing and capitalization when transliterating into English is arbitrary. In general, one word per kanji, except when the kanji form a clear compound: Oi Zuki not Oizuki but Gedan not Ge Dan or Ge-dan.

❧ ❧ ❧

Following the Japanese, which lacks grammatical number, we usually use the same form for singular and plural: one kata, two kata; a karateka, some karateka; 1 samurai, 2 samurai. Otherwise, we treat the Japanese jargon once introduced as though it were English, without italicization.

❧ ❧ ❧

There are many ways to write Japanese in the Roman alphabet we use in English, none of which is entirely satisfactory. We follow a modified version of the Hepburn System, except when quoting, we use the form and spelling in the original. In direct quotes, the author's words are reproduced exactly as written unless indicated in [brackets]. You consequently might see different renderings of the same word. Get used to it, there are differences from source to source as an unavoidable result of transliterating words from a totally unrelated language into English. When we can determine it, we spell names in the way people spell them themselves. For an author, we use the spelling from the title page of the book. So Ohtsuka not Ōtsuka.

❧ ❧ ❧

Those unfamiliar with spoken Japanese find macrons (ō, ū) distracting, but they are essential to correct pronunciation. As a compromise, we generally show the macrons on the first or defining occurrence of a word, and in the sections aimed at those interested in the language. We don't put the macrons in words and names that are recognized by most English speakers, so Tokyo not Tōkyō and Osaka not Ōsaka. We do this out of our great concern for the reader, and because it's easier to leave them off and we're lazy.

❧ ❧ ❧

There are as many variations within the Hepburn System as there are variations in techniques between the various styles. When faced with a choice, we chose the form easiest to pronounce by the reader unfamiliar with Japanese. For example, we use Empi not Enpi, Zuki not Dzuki, and dojo not doujou, although we will often point out alternatives as we go along.

❧ ❧ ❧

We use British, or more accurately, "International" quotes. North Americans put punctuation inside quotes whether it logically belongs there or not, for a reason having to do with the inferiority of American typesetting equipment. America is no longer inferior and we don't even typeset, so we place punctuation in the most logical way.

❧ ❧ ❧

Wadō Ki Kai ® is a registered trademark of the Wadō Ki Kai Karate system, developed by John Pereira, and currently headed by Sensei Ferol Arce. For ease of reading, we do not repeat the registration mark throughout the text, but assert the trademark nonetheless.

I.

GROUND: The Taikyoku

The Foundation

This is probably the only book on Karate written by a Master and a Beginner, a high-ranking Black Belt and a low-level White Belt. The Black Belt brings the perspective of years of experience, the White Belt brings the Beginner's Mind. We will share with you precepts of a master, insights of a beginner, and some Japanese and Okinawan lore and language picked up because of a life-long fascination with Things Japanese.

We've put together this book on the Taikyoku kata for karateka—practitioners of Karate—at all levels. We hope it will serve as a useful reference as well as provide some entertainment. We hope you will find this book, and your study of Karate, to be an interesting and rewarding journey.

Sen Ri no Michi mo Ippo kara
"Even a Journey of a Thousand Miles starts from One Step"

This is a familiar kotowaza, or proverb, meaning you have to start somewhere. In Wadō Ki Kai, we start with the Taikyoku kata, studied by White Belts on their way to Yellow. In Japan, the color white is associated with transition—to embark upon a new field of knowledge with no preconceived notions or presuppositions. In this sense, the white belt karateka portrays the vastest potential of all karateka in the ranking system, for the white belt is a symbol of all that can possibly be achieved. Some ryū, or styles of Karate, prefer to skip Taikyoku and start with the Pingan or Pinan kata, also called Heian, which we in Wadō Ki Kai, or WKK for short, learn as yellow and orange belts. Styles that do use Taikyoku kata do them as the first kata learned. So it's up to you, take that first step.

The Taikyoku Kata

From the large, you can know the small; and from the shallow you can understand the deep. The chapter is called Ground and it will ground you for the rest of the book.
　　—Miyamoto Musashi, describing Chi no Rin, the Ring of Ground.

Although the exact beginnings of Karate are somewhat uncertain, a combination of archeological evidence, written documentation, and oral history shows us that what we today call "Karate" is Okinawan. Records indicate that the Okinawans combined several Chinese boxing styles with their own indigenous systems. Karate was not introduced to the rest of the world until the great Okinawan Karate master, Gichin Funakoshi, first introduced it in Japan in the 1920's.

Called the "Father of Modern Karate", Funakoshi moved from Okinawa to Tokyo where he promoted Karate and developed it into the art we practice today. Karate underwent a scientific revolution in Japan. All available knowledge in the study of anatomy, the laws of physics and human psychology were applied for its further research and development in Japan. And, today, what is called modern Karate is the result of this study.

Funakoshi had published poetry under a pen name, Shōtō, so his students named his dojo Shōtōkan, kan meaning *hall*. The Shōtōkan houses the Japan Karate Association (JKA). Funakoshi was encouraged in this effort by Jigorō Kanō (1860-1938) founder of the Kōdōkan, where modern Jūdō was developed. Funakoshi adapted many of Kano's ideas to Karate, including the Gi and Belt system, and developed a distinctive regimen for Karate training. The Taikyoku Kata were a part of his regimen. Funakoshi invented the Taikyoku Kata, aided by his son Gigo Funakoshi (1906-1945), and introduced them in his book *Karate-dō Kyōhan*: "In addition to these [various historical] kata, I have, as a result of several years of research into the general problem, developed two sets of kata, the Taikyoku no Kata, for beginners, and the Ten no Kata, to be used as matching (kumite) forms."[1] He explains: "Since this form is the easiest of the kata to learn and consists of those blocks and attacks that are the most helpful in practicing basic techniques, it should be the form with which beginners start."[2]

Taikyoku doesn't always get the respect it deserves. McCarthy calls Taikyoku kihon—what WKK calls Shinkokata, or Drilling Movements—not kata, and says kihon are, "Various basic formal beginner exercises, including gekki sai, taikyo ku, and fukyu."[3] And Grupp implies they might not be considered kata at all: "In Shotokan, there are 26 kata if one does not count the Taikyoku-Kata preliminary exercise forms."[4] Although Ohshima is not overly impressed with Taikyoku himself, he does allow that others see its benefit: "A few of my senior students think that the Taikyoku katas are very important to practice although I don't lead them very much. Master Egami, one of my most respected seniors, felt that the Taikyoku katas were the ideal form and should be practiced the most."[5]

But Pierre Blot sees Taikyoku as quite valuable: "The pattern and techniques are very basic and consist of two or three movements repeated throughout the form. The repetition enables you to keep a clear mind and to concentrate on the balance of each stance and the power of your blocks and counterattacks. Each taikyoku consists of twenty movements evolving along the same set pattern. The direction of the movements and the turns remain the same."[6]

"On the Composition of this Book in 5 Rings"

This book has been arranged into five chapters, roughly paralleling the organization of Miyamoto Musashi's *Go Rin no Sho, The Book of Five Rings*. The first chapter covers foundation concepts, and each of the other four chapters covers one of the four kata in the Taikyoku series. Each chapter will have several sections; their order will vary a little for exposition. First in Chapter 1 for the Taikyoku series, then for each individual kata in the following chapters, we will have various sections:

Kata Choreography

A **kata** is a *form* for practicing and demonstrating Karate techniques. The moves for each kata are presented in a chart. As a karateka, you will perform kata many times. The procedure is to bow before beginning the kata. The performer should always announce the name of the kata before the performance, then perform the kata. Announce the name of the kata, then bow and end in Shizentai. We call this section Choreography in recognition of the similarity between kata and dance, noted by many practitioners, including some of the old Okinawan masters.

In this section, we simply list in chart form the moves and sequences of the kata. You'll want to use this section in conjunction with the Wadō Ki Kai website at www.wadokikai.com. You'll actually be able to see the kata performed by Sensei Arce, step through it, or stop motion to study any position.

Shinkokata

The moves for the shinkokata are presented in a chart. **Shinkokata** are the basic techniques which accompany each kata. They are exercises performed by the class as a group to practice the fundamental techniques, and are called *kihon* in some styles. They consist of blocks, parries, strikes, kicks, punches, etc., which make up the moves of Karate. The longer a student trains, the more complex and demanding the shinkokatas become.

Shinkokata 1-3 are in Zenkutsu Dachi, Shinkokata 4 is in Kamae. The four shinkokata each take one movement from each of the Taikyoku kata. They each have two kiai, same as the Taikyoku Kata.

1. From Taikyoku Shodan: Oi Zuki
2. From Taikyoku Nidan: Age Uke
3. From Taikyoku Sandan: Gamen Shutō
4. From Taikyoku Yodan: Mae Geri

Here's the drill (literally): All the shinkokata have the same form. On the command "Hajime", assume the starting position. For the first three, the starting position is Gedan Barai, for Shinkokata 4, just assume the starting position, Kamae. Then by the numbers, do the practice waza, or technique, five times, with a kiai on the fifth (last) technique of each line. On the command "Kaesu", turn around to the left (counterclockwise) into the starting position. Do the waza five times again, again with a kiai. On the command "Kaesu", turn 180 degrees into starting position. On "Yame", go to Shizentai, or natural position, unless commanded to repeat the drill.

Note the lack of balance: each technique is executed on the right six times, on the left only four. The 180° turns are counterclockwise, opposite of the 180° turns in the kata.

Technique

For each kata, there will be a section for each new technique, in the order they occur. Taikyoku kata appear in several ryū, or styles. There is disagreement from style to style over how many Taikyoku Kata there are, and variation in their contents. Funakoshi shows three. WKK has four Taikyoku Kata. Yamaguchi has five. Pierre Blot says there are six. Sources agree on what the moves are in Shodan,[7] but there are several versions of Nidan and Sandan, and no source for Yodan. We'll point out the variations from WKK as we go along, but suffice it to say the WKK versions contain a greater variety of techniques, and a better sampling, than the other ryu. Although we concentrate on Wadō Ki Kai, we also show variations in case you are unfortunately from a different style (just kidding).

Training Notes

For each technique there is a section with Training Notes, or keys to understanding the techniques, where we've collected lists of things a beginner needs to keep in mind to improve performance of the kata, in the spirit of Bruce Lee's *Tao of Jeet Kune Do*,[8] with more or less random notes collected about each technique. Hey, if it was okay for Bruce, why not for us? Of course, Bruce had a pretty good excuse for not polishing his notes—he was dead at the time. His wife, Linda Lee Cadwell, used his unfinished notes as the basis for the book. Your list of training notes might be different, but will probably overlap ours quite a bit. Think of these as themes you might focus on during a repetition of the kata. For example, you might run through the kata concentrating on keeping your stance low down the center.

Kumite

Kumite or *sparring* is a way of practicing Karate techniques with a partner. There are two primary types of kumite: pre-arranged (yakusoku), and free (ju). Although the WKK school does not emphasize sport karate, sparring is an important aspect of our training in the development of technique, attitude, coordination, distance, and judgment.

Since this book is for beginners, most chapters do not have a section on Kumite.

Dojo Lore

In this section we try to include useful and interesting knowledge for the karateka in the dojo. Dōjō means literally "Place of the Way", so it's the place, in the sense of a building, in which the Karate classes are conducted. But the dojo is more than just a building; it's perfectly possible to have a dojo with no regular meeting place. In this sense the dojo is the concept of the group of students and teachers following the Way together. The Way they are following is the Dō of Karate-Dō, as some practitioners prefer to call Karate. Dō has deep philosophical implications, but for now we'll leave it unexplained, and revisit it in Chapter 3.

Karate Controversy

As a professional Systems Analyst, Patrick has always been interested in systems and how they work, and particularly how the human mind comprehends systems. Controversy is always a fascinating aspect of how systems are viewed, understood and transmitted, so we try to be controversial whenever possible. Like all other human systems, Karate has much controversy over matters great and small. We'll point out some of these as we go along, and sometimes express an opinion. If you don't agree, don't get upset. Our purpose is to provide some material for discussions over coffee or beers, not to expound the final answer to these questions.

Philosophy

Some of you might be interested in Japanese philosophy. Karate has deep roots in Asian philosophy, and we'll try to introduce you to some of it in these sections. If you're new to these concepts, give them a try and let them sink in.

Nihongo

We've called this section *Nihongo*, which means "the Japanese language" in the Japanese language. In this section, we'll discuss the language, Japanese words and phrases, and pronunciation. Since some of you might not be interested in Japanese, we've designed the book such that it is possible for you to skip these sections, or proceed more slowly through them, as you see fit. As a consequence, there might be some repetition in this section, but if you're just beginning in Japanese, that's a feature, not a bug, as computer programmers are wont to say.

We'll also try to teach elementary Japanese pronunciation. Japanese is pronounced quite differently from English. If you've ever tried to understand a Japanese accent you can be sure your Japanese sounds worse than that. First, bolster your confidence. Most English speakers pronounce most, if not all, Japanese words incorrectly, so if you do, too, you'll fit right in at an American dojo. If you go to Japan, however, some polishing will be a very good idea. Long vowels especially will need attention.

It is quite common for there to be a pair of entirely different words with the difference of a long vowel. A friend of mine visiting his teacher tried to say: "Your children are so cute!", but instead said: "Your children are pitiful!" Seward relates the embarrassment of a man who confounded "assistant" (komon) with "anus" (kōmon) with predictably unfortunate results.[9] It's always dangerous to make generalizations, but by and large, karateka who have risen to the rank of Assistant Teacher tend to be overly status-conscious. When they become full-fledged teachers, they are confident in themselves, and will give you the benefit of the doubt over an honest mistake. But Assistants are still a little insecure, and feel they need to prove something. So it's probably *not* a good idea to call the Assistant Teacher an asshole. It's probably also a good idea to not tell any karateka his or her children are pitiful, unless you happen to be looking for a particularly spirited sparring match that day. And take our advice: Never even try to talk about a cute Assistant!

Taikyoku Technique

Embusen

The pattern, or line of movement, outlined on the floor by the karateka while doing a kata is called *embusen*. The embusen for all the Taikyoku trace a pattern similar to the Roman numeral one, or the letter 'I'. In Japanese it traces the kanji for the word kō, so is called the Kō Embusen. Funakoshi explains the embusen for all the Taikyoku kata: "The Taikyoku forms consist of units, with blocks followed by single front attacks along Lines 1 and 3, or blocks followed by three continuous front attacks along Line 2, each form having altogether twenty movements."[10]

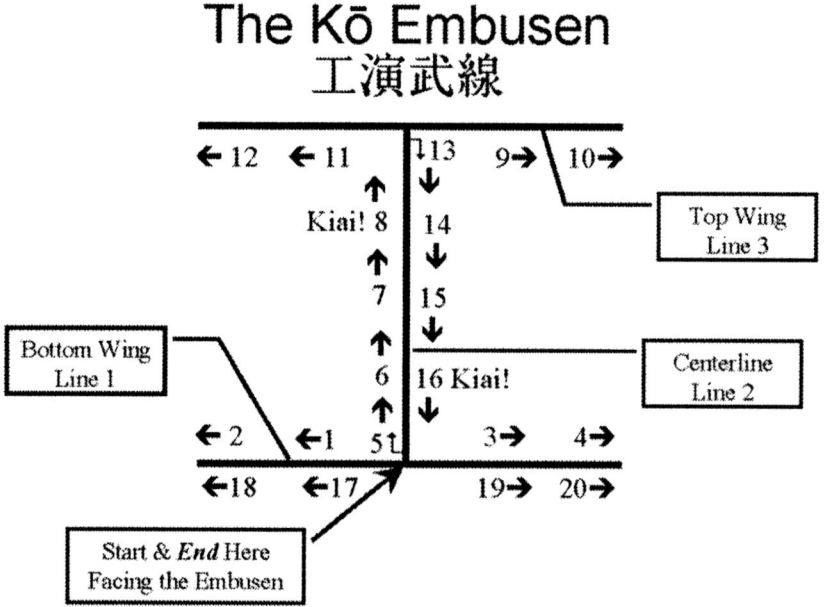

Note that each kata starts and ends at same spot on the floor. This shows consistency of stance. Like life, a kata makes a circle: for example, we start and end life bald, toothless, and helpless.

(Over) Analysis of Taikyoku

Sorry, but Patrick's careers as both an economic analyst and then a systems analyst cause him to sometimes over-analyze things. The random observations we present in this section might help you remember the moves. Or might confuse you beyond recovery.

Here's what you'll have learned when you know all four Taikyoku kata:

Blocks: 3 Uke—Age Uke, Ude Uke, Uraken Uke.
(plus Gedan Barai, which is in a class by itself)
Hand techniques: 3 Te-waza—Seiken, Shutō, Uraken.
Kick: 1 Keri—Mae Geri.
Punches: 3 Tsuki—Gyaku Zuki, Oi Zuki, Yoko Zuki.
Stances: 3 Tachi—Zenkutsu Dachi, Kiba Dachi, Kōkutsu Dachi.
Strikes: 2 Uchi—Shutō Uchi and Uraken Uchi.
Sweep: 1 Harai—Gedan Barai, the all-purpose cool move.

The kata follow a performance line, or embusen. All four kata follow the same embusen or pattern, the Kō Embusen, like the Roman numeral I.

All four kata have the same count of actions, twenty, if you count each combination as one action.

On each wing, the top and bottom line of the I or Kō, you perform the same techniques twice, once on each side. Each half is a mirror image of the other. Wings are done three times, for a total of six repetitions of each technique, three on each side. Within each kata, all three wings are the same.

Both centerlines are the same within a given kata. They are NOT mirror images, but identical, thus the right and left sides do not get an identical workout. Consider Shodan. Since all stances are Zenkutsu, and the kata begins and ends at the same spot, there are necessarily exactly the same number of Zenkutsu on the left as the right. But you do two extra Gedan Barai on the left, and two extra tsuki on the right. That's 5 left, 3 right Gedan Barai, and 5 left, 7 right Oi Zuki, for a total of 10 actions on each side.

Within each kata, the techniques are performed three times down each centerline, twice on the right and once on the left. The centerline is done twice, for a total of six repetitions, four on the right and two on the left.

In all four kata, a kiai shout should be heard at the end of moves 8 and 16, and at no other time.

All turns are *into* the embusen, never away
All the turns occur at the same place on the embusen
In each kata, 90° turns are done 2 times, in moves 5 & 13
All 90° turns are Counterclockwise
In each kata, 180° turns are done 3 times, in moves 3, 11 & 19
All 180° turns are Clockwise
In each kata, 270° turns are done 2 times, in moves 9 & 17
All 270° turns are Counterclockwise

A little numb from all this analysis? Hey, don't blame us. We warned you it was an *over*-analysis!

Variations on Taikyoku Kata

In this book, we'll of course favor Wadō Ki Kai but will try to cover the other styles, some of which are (almost ☺) as good as WKK.

Yamaguchi shows five kata (actually, each kata has a variation so you could say there are ten), called Jodan, Chudan and Gedan, plus Kake-Uke and Mawashi Uke. Note the first three kata are also named using dan, or level, but instead of the skill level of the karateka, they are classed by the delivery level of the technique. The names mean upper-level, midlevel and lower-level, and the techniques block and attack according to the level of the name. Goju's Taikyoku Gedan has the same techniques in the same order as our Taikyoku Shodan, although the stance is different (see Variations on Shodan in Chapter 2).

Dojo Lore

Opening Class

When class is called to order by the Sensei, students are expected to line up quickly, quietly, and respectfully. Do not talk while lining up. The order of the line-up should be according to rank, and each rank should be ordered by height. The instructor(s) will begin the class by kneeling. The senior student will say the word, "**mokusō**". It refers to the meditation phase of the opening, which lasts about one minute. Use it to clear your mind and prepare for the class ahead. "Yame" is the signal to end the meditation.

In our school, after everyone has knelt down and mokuso has finished, there are three deep bows from the seated or kneeling position:

1. **Shōmen ni rei**   Bowing to the ideals and traditions of our school.
2. **Sensei ni rei**   Bowing to the teacher(s). Those who are here to help us learn and to share their knowledge with us.
3. **Otagai ni rei**   Bowing to one another as an acknowledgement that we are all students of the martial arts, and that we all can learn from one another.

Always bow respectfully as you enter and leave the dojo. You show respect for the dojo, the art, your fellow students, and the instructors by doing so. If a class has already begun, quietly bow in at the door, enter the room, and step to the side, be seated and perform the opening ceremony silently to yourself. You may join the class at this point, as long as they too have finished the formal class bow in.

Counting

Japanese language topics are normally covered in Nihongo, but everyone needs to know basic counting, since exercises and kata are counted that way. We'll use the numbers to sneak in a little basic pronunciation. Numbers in Japan can even be a commodity, as in the case of the telephone system. To get a telephone connection, you have to tell the telephone company what the telephone number will be. No kidding, the telephone company has no telephone numbers. You have to buy a number from someone; some numbers are very expensive, and others very cheap. For example, the number four can be pronounced "shi", which also means "death". So a number with a lot of fours is a bad number indeed, and cheap. Eight, on the other hand, means "wealth", so only a wealthy person could afford all eights. The Japanese language has a limited number of possible syllables, and multiple pronunciations for most words, including numbers, one from aboriginal Japanese and one from Chinese, so it's usually easy to make a phrase out of a number, like on vanity license plates. Clever phrases are worth a lot. This system apparently dates back to the original phone system in the 1920s. Politicians were given blocks of phone numbers in return for favorable votes, bureaucrats were given numbers for favorable decisions; since no money or tangible property was involved it didn't meet the legal definition of a bribe. But now no one who owns an expensive number wants to end the system.

#	Count
1	Ichi
2	Ni
3	San
4	Shi or Yon
5	Go
6	Roku
7	Shichi or Nana
8	Hachi
9	Ku or Kyū
10	Jū

1 Ichi

In Spanish and Italian, yes is si, "see". The i sounds like the English name of the letter 'E'. Kata Jion is "gee own". And the number one is actually "ee chee", or "each", but not "itchy", although not as easy to remember, nor as catchy, so we'll give you itchy if you'll work hard on the other numbers: shichi (7) is "She Chee" not "Shitchee".

2 Ni

This one's easy. Pronounced like "knee", the 'I' sounding like a long e in English.

3 San

The A is pronounced "Ah", so sahn, rhymes with John, not like in sand. When someone says Sankyu, don't say "You're welcome". They're telling you that person has a Third Kyu Brown Belt.

4 Shi or Yon

You've probably heard four counted as "She". Four can be either *shi* or *yon*. Shi is sometimes superstitiously avoided because it can also mean *death*. It also sounds too much like seven, shichi, which sounds like "sheetch" when said loud or fast.

5 Go

This one should go easy: just like the English word "go". Go is also the name of a very complicated game, the object of which is to get five tokens in a row, hence the name. It would seem a simple game, since on the surface it's an extension of Tic-Tac-Toe, but that's deceiving. It's much more complex than chess, for example, because the number of possibilities per move is much greater. Feng-Hsiung Hsu, who was behind the IBM computer that defeated Gary Kasparov, says in *Behind Deep Blue*, speaking of what might be the next challenge for computers: "Among games with perfect information (games that do not depend on chance events like coin flips, die rolls or card shuffling), 'Go' is generally recognized as the most difficult game. It is probably sufficiently difficult that it will not be 'solved' within the next 20 years."[11]

6 Roku

The first syllable is "row". The U sounds like oo, as in "Oo wee, baby", or "boo". Never include a 'y' sound, unless a y is written there. So the ku is coo, not like in "Cutey-Pie", which would be kyu. This is sometimes confused because the number 9 can be pronounced either ku or kyu; that is a coincidence—ku and kyu are not otherwise interchangeable.

7 Shichi

Sometimes the I is dropped at the end, so shichi (7) can be either "she chee" or "sheetch" (but rhymes with "each", not "switch"). For similar reasons to four, seven has an alternate, *nana*.

8 Hachi

Sometimes the I is dropped at the end, so hachi (8) can be "ha chee" or "hahtch"—like "hot" with a ch added. It does not sound like "hatch".

9 Ku or Kyū

Coo like a baby, or pool cue with the u held longer. Either is acceptable, and a matter of personal taste.

10 Jū

Pronounced like "Jew", but hold the oo sound a little longer. Okinawans sometimes use "sei" for ten, so Seisan is 13 and Niseishiho is the same as Nijushiho, 24 steps.

Taikyoku Controversy

A showdown on Shodan: Who is the inventor of the Kata? There are three claimants to invention of the Taikyoku kata, Funakoshi (1868-1957), Miyagi (1888-1953), and Nagamine (1907-1997).

Who-Done-It Controversy

As we have seen, Funakoshi claimed to be the developer of the Taikyoku in his 1936 book, where he says: "This form [another form, Ten no Kata] was introduced along with the Taikyoku Kata over ten years ago by the author."[12]

The style Gōjū Ryū also has a kata series called Taikyoku. Gosei Yamaguchi has written a book, *Goju-Ryu Karate II*, which is largely devoted to Goju's Taikyoku, which has some variation from our source authors. Yamaguchi refers to the Taikyoku as part of the Fukyu Gata (Universal Exercise Kata), but he does not attribute the kata to Gichin Funakoshi in the 1920s. Instead he says it was developed in the 1940s by Chojun Miyagi[13] (Remember, from the movie *The Karate Kid*: it's "Me Yah Ghee", not "Me Yah Jee"!). Shoshin Nagamine in *The Essence of Okinawan Karate-Do* claims to have been the co-developer of the Fukyugata kata with Miyagi.[14] Nagamine details two Fukyugata, the second of which has similarities with the WKK Taikyoku Shodan and Nidan.

Curious, that people would develop such similar kata with the same name if there were no connection. Funakoshi's book was apparently published at least five years before the Fukyu Gata was developed, and claims that the kata were developed ten years earlier, so it would seem Funakoshi must have been first. And getting curiouser and curiouser, Yamaguchi makes this statement:

> Taikyoku is the Japanese pronunciation of the Chinese character for tai chi. This doesn't necessarily mean there is any relationship between the Taikyoku kata and tai chi other than the fact that both titles refer to the relationship between the four major universal directions, North, South, East and West.
>
> Thus, master Chojun Miyagi chose to instruct his students that the Chinese characters should be spelled out phonetically rather than literally, in the hope of avoiding confusion.[15]

It's a curious statement because if he invented the kata, couldn't he have named it whatever he wanted? He could have called it the Purple-Passion Kata, or the Super-Duper-Razzle-Dazzle Kata, or even the Kata-Whose-Name-Should-Be-Ignored. Why would he choose a name and then tell his students it has no significance, ignore it? It seems to support the theory the kata were actually adapted from the earlier Funakoshi kata. Then again, the name Gōjū Ryū means *Hard Soft Style*, so contradiction is part of their name. Maybe this is just another Zen-like contradiction within the style.

Taikyoku Philosophy

The Name Taikyoku

The name Taikyoku is composed of two kanji, or Japanese characters, the first meaning *Great*, the second meaning *Extremes* or *Poles*. You may say "Taikyoku Kata" or "Taikyoku no Kata". The *no* is the equivalent of an *'s* in English, and as with its English equivalent it is optional in many phrases. Taikyoku is often translated The Great Limit, but is also called the Ultimate Extremity, Grand Ultimate, or the *Supreme Ultimate*, as we called it in the title of this book. The kanji for

Taikyoku are pronounced "T'ai Chi" in Chinese. T'ai Chi is both a slow-motion martial art and a name for the Yin-Yang Symbol. The name Taikyoku draws deeply on Esoteric Asian philosophy. Funakoshi in *Kyōhan* calls it "First cause". In his book *Notes on Training*, Tsutomu Ohshima says "Taikyoku means first cause or the original force in the universe before there was any form."[16] Tadashi Nakamura says Taikyoku "Means taking the overview, the large view. See the whole rather than focusing on the individual parts."[17] Manuel Adrogué calls Taikyoku, *Tae Kuk* in Korean, the Great Principle—"According to Daoism, the underlying principle of existence."[18] And Genwa Nakasone says Taikyoku kata is the "kata of the beginning of the universe".[19] In WKK, Taikyoku is interpreted as "The focusing and synchronization of the vast elements of mind, body and spirit", which is not a literal translation, but is the best philosophical explanation of the term you'll find. If this is your first taste of Asian philosophy, simply keep this interpretation in mind.

Taikyoku is in fact a deep philosophical term. D.T. Suzuki quotes Ichiun, speaking of Taikyoku: "In order to explain the mysterious working of Heavenly Reason or of the Primary Nature in man, we make use of various expressions, but the main thing is to return to the innocence of the original man, that is, of infancy, which is often called Great Limit (taikyoku; t'ai chi in Chinese), or Nature in its isness, or a state of no-action or emptiness. But most people, instead of looking directly into the fact, cling to words and their commentaries and go on entangling themselves further and further, finally putting themselves into an inextricable snare."[20] Perhaps we can get out of this snare with some help from one of the Greatest Writers of all time, Miyamoto Musashi.

Miyamoto Musashi

Miyamoto Musashi (1584-1645) is honored as "The Sword Saint", and is considered one of Japan's greatest martial arts strategists. His masterwork, *Go Rin no Sho, The Book of Five Rings*—written for his sword fighting students shortly before his death—is divided into five subdivisions (rings or scrolls). Our book loosely follows a similar organizing theme. Each ring, or chapter, is named for one of the five elements of Esoteric Buddhist alchemy. Musashi was not only a martial artist, but an artist of image (two of his works, including his self-portrait shown here, are included in this book) and word as well. Musashi is one of our heroes, not as much for his martial arts feats as for his writing. He is, after all, one of the most successful authors in history. To still be in print after 350 years is an accomplishment few authors can hope to achieve. His book has been translated into every major language, and he currently has at least ten translations in print in English alone. If you are really serious about learning martial arts, you should get a copy of his book. Note the name is given as Miyamoto Musashi, Japanese style, or Musahi Miyamoto, Western style.

In *Go Rin no Sho*, the Sword Master enumerates principles of strategy. These precepts have surprisingly broad application to systems analysis and business, as well as martial arts. Although he was actually a master of Kendō, the Way of the Sword, *Time* Magazine called Musashi "Japan's answer to the Harvard MBA!" *Time* went on to say: "On Wall Street, when Musashi talks, people listen."

A Book of Five Rings

Miyamoto Musashi's *Go Rin no Sho*, *The Book of Five Rings*, is essential for every martial arts library. My homeboy (from Oakland) Thomas Cleary has a translation out in a pocket version by Shambhala Pocket Classics for $7.00, so you can't use price as an excuse.[21] Cleary is an Asian scholar; you might prefer one by a fellow budoka. Interpretations by martial artists include D.E Tarver's, Hidy Ochiai's, and Stephen Kaufmann's. Here are the three books, with biographic material taken from the books themselves.

> Miyamoto Musashi, D. E. **Tarver**, trans., *The Book of Five Rings*, San Jose: Writers Club Press, 2002 (1643). ISBN: 0-595-23006-7. "Tarver holds black belts ranging from 2nd to 7th degree in seven different styles of Japanese and Filipino martial arts." He has done a series of interpretations of Asian warrior classics like this one, such as Sun Tzu's *Art of War*. $10.95.

> **Kaufman**, Stephen F., *The Martial Artist's Book of Five Rings*, Boston: Tuttle Publishing, 1994. ISBN: 0-8048-3020-7. Steve Kaufman is "Hanshi 10th Dan", founder of Dojo no Hebi, the School of the Snake, in New York City. $12.95.

> **Ochiai**, Hidy, *A Way to Victory: The Annotated Book of Five Rings*, Woodstock, New York: The Overlook Press, 2001. ISBN: 1-58567-038-3. Includes considerable interesting commentary by Professor (of Anthropology at SUNY) Ohiai. Hidy Ochiai has been inducted into the Black Belt Hall of Fame. His other books include *The Complete Book of Self-Defense*. $29.95.

Musashi's Nine Principles

Since this chapter is themed on the Ring of Ground, we, like Musashi, conclude the chapter with the Nine Principles:[22]

Musashi's Nine Principles

1. Think of what is right and true.
2. The Way is in training.
3. Cultivate a wide range of interests in the arts.
4. Know the Ways of all occupations.
5. Understand Economics*—Profit & Loss.
6. Develop and trust your intuition.
7. Perceive that which cannot be seen with the eye.
8. Pay attention even to trifles.
9. Do not do anything useless.

Musashi: "First of all, train in martial arts with these principles in your mind. You must be able to see what's immediately in front of you in its larger context. If you master strategy, you can win against twenty or even thirty opponents. If you exert yourself in the right Way, you can defeat others not only with your technique, but with your perception. When your body moves freely, at will, you can defeat others physically. And if your mind is trained the same way, you can defeat others mentally. With such abilities, how could you lose?"

Nihongo

The Nihongo section at the end of each chapter will be optional, since many people interested in Karate are not necessarily interested in Japanese. You might at least read the first section covering pronunciation, since this is the area where English speakers are worst.

The Devil's Tongue

Jack Seward tells of a Catholic missionary attempting to convert the Japanese to Christianity who reported to Rome he was having great difficulty learning the language. He concluded the Japanese language was a plot by Satan to prevent him from preaching successfully.[23] And here, we'll try to teach you to pronounce the Devil's Tongue.

---

* Okay, it's anachronistic, but Musashi would have used the term if Economics had been invented in 1643.

It's better to pronounce correctly, but if you aren't sure, just do your best. One thing that might reduce your embarrassment is the fact Japanese has several very different dialects, including the Okinawan dialect, called Hogen (sometimes Hogan), which means even Japanese have trouble pronouncing Japanese correctly.

Okinawa's Hogen Dialect

Gichin Funakoshi was a schoolteacher in Okinawa who was chosen to demonstrate Karate to distinguished visitors, including Crown Prince Hirohito, the future Emperor. Strange as it sounds, he was chosen not because his Karate was the best, but because his Japanese was. The Okinawan dialect is quite different from Modern Standard Japanese (MSJ) as spoken in the Tokyo region, as demonstrated by the difference in pronunciation of the exact same word "Pingan" in Okinawa, as "Heian" in Tokyo. Okinawan also has a syllable, Fa, that does not occur in MSJ, so the kata Saifa and Naifanchi sometimes become Saiha and Naihanchi in MSJ. Okinawan speakers will sometimes have subtitled captions in movies and on TV because mainland Japanese can't understand the dialect. A bilingual schoolmate of Patrick's from Okinawa went to visit his cousins in Tokyo and greeted them in Japanese, but in the Okinawan dialect. His cousins were irritated with him: "Don't be a showoff, you speak English and we don't, so don't embarrass us by speaking English." They thought Okinawan Japanese was English! So if you're talking to a Japanese from Tokyo, imply you have an Okinawan accent and vice versa; they might think you're speaking perfect Japanese with a regional accent.

Consonants

Consonants can appear only at the beginning of syllables, not the end. As a result, words of English origin mysteriously gain syllables when they enter Japanese. One of the most difficult words to learn in Japanese is Makudonarudo, "Ma Coo Dough Nah Rue Dough". It is the name of a very popular place to eat in Japan—It is the closest a Japanese can come to saying the word "McDonalds".*
Another example is "strike", which is used in Japanese baseball and labor relations. The word became *sutoraiku* in Japanese, "Sue Toe Rah Ee Cue"—one English syllable becomes *five* in Japanese.

---

* A Japanese Boy Scout returning from a Jamboree in America was asked by a reporter for his impression of the US. He said it wasn't all that exotic: "It's a lot like Japan. They even have McDonalds there"!

James C. Hepburn, MD, the medical missionary who devised the system that forms the basis of most systems for writing Japanese for Westerners, including the one used in this book, chose to transliterate the consonants as in English. So as an English speaker, your consonants will be good if you remember just one rule: the G is always hard, so mae geri (front kick) sounds like "My Gary" not "My Jerry". The F and the R are a little different (if you are familiar with the French or Spanish R sound, use it), the N sometimes is (like the French nasal N), and there is a consonant sound, Ts, that is problematical, but for now you'll do fine if you just pronounce the consonants as in English.

Vowels

The most important aspect of your pronunciation of Japanese is the vowels. If you are an English speaker, there is good news and bad news. First, the bad news: The pronunciation of vowels is very different in English and Japanese. But the good news: once you learn the vowels in Japanese, you'll know them in virtually every other language in the world, including Italian, French, Spanish, and even the Polynesian languages—Patrick was once complimented on his near-native Hawaiian, when all he had done was pronounce the unfamiliar Hawaiian names as if they were Japanese! It can be confusing, since E is pronounced 'A', I is pronounced 'E', and A is pronounced like a short O. (Strangely enough, the O is actually pronounced 'O'!) This peculiarity is caused not because Japanese is perverse, but because English is—English is different from all the other languages that use the Roman alphabet. As in the French merci, pronounced "mare see", the E sounds like the English name of the letter 'A', and the I like an English 'E'.

Let's look at the vowels in a little more detail. If you're not a native English speaker, you probably won't need examples since your native language pronunciation will match the Japanese. You'll often see examples from Standard American English in this book, usually put in double quotes, so for example the Japanese word *dan* is pronounced "Don". As England and the U.S.A. are two nations divided by a common language, the examples are sure to work only if pronounced as in America. If you're from England, you should try pronouncing your English better, anyway. Hey, if we Americans are speaking English real good, why ain't you?

The good Dr. Hepburn, alas, chose to transliterate the vowels as in Italian. The English vowels actually can take on the Japanese (or Italian) pronunciation, as shown in the list below. As we go along, we'll point out cases where novices make mistakes, so no need to memorize the table, just familiarize yourself with it:

A	as in Father
E	as in Merit; or internally as in Met
I	as in Marine
O	as in No
U	as in Rule

E is the worst for English speakers, because it's so easy to say it like the English E. The alcoholic beverage made from rice is saké, "sah kay", not "socky". Sake does not rhyme with stocky. A Japanese beauty might be a geisha, "gay sha", not a "ghee sha". The second syllable in uke (block) is "kay", not "key", which has the disadvantage of sounding too much like uchi (strike), in addition to meaning *rainy season*, not *block*. E can sometimes sound like a short e, however, especially in desu, which pretty much means 'is', depending on what the meaning of 'is' is, as an American President once said. Desu usually rhymes with "bless", as in "I'll never learn this blessed kata!", the u being (almost) silent. In addition to the vowels there are semi-vowels, and we'll look at the Ns of Embusen as the first of these.

Phonetic Shift N->M

Embusen, the pattern made on the floor by the karateka doing a kata, literally means the *performing warrior line*, the *em* being the character for a performance in an act or play, the *bu* being the same bu meaning warrior or military in Budō and Bushidō, and the *sen* being *line* as in a line in geometry or a subway line. It is also the sen of Shinkansen, which is called in English the Bullet Train. Disappointingly, the name literally means "the New Trunk Line", a name that does not invoke the visions of sleek speed we get in the English Bullet Train.

You will also see e<u>m</u>busen written e<u>n</u>busen, with an N instead of an M, but it should be pronounced like an M whichever way it's written. This is a phonetic shift, the same shift that makes the sen of sensei become sem in sempai. First, this letter is actually more like a vowel than a consonant, so linguists call it a semi-vowel. The character is actually a full syllable unto itself, so embusen has *five* syllables: E M Bu Se N; not three: Em Bu Sen. Most English speakers have trouble with this N, which is similar to the French nasal N. In any event, this N sound shifts to what sounds like an M before Bs, Ps, and Ms, and sometimes in other places as well. Note this is a difference in English, there is no change in written Japanese, since a Japanese naturally does the shift without even thinking of it as a shift. This is similar to shifts in English, as when the T in *invent* is pronounced 'ch' in *invention*. Japanese Studies scholars don't like to change the letter to M since there is no change in written Japanese, so they leave it N even though it is pronounced M. The weapon called the Nunchaku can also sound like Numchaku, as this same semi-vowel either does or doesn't shift to an M. Karate teaches us to avoid a fight when possible, so maybe you should simply call them "Chucks", thus avoiding the issue of the N/M semi-vowel entirely in this case.

Taikyoku Kanji

To start, you need to understand a bit about Japanese writing, called kanji. At first kanji characters look like what Murray & Wong call *Noodle Words*,[24] since to the untrained eye, they look as meaningful as a plate of spaghetti. Unfortunately for the Japanese, they were near to China and took the Chinese writing system, called kanji. This was unfortunate because Japanese and Chinese are entirely different languages. In fact, English is closer to either language than they are to each other, so as bad as Americans are at Japanese, the Chinese are even worse!! Chinese is a tonal monosyllabic positional-syntax language and Japanese is monotonal, polysyllabic and inflected, which is the academic way of saying it was a match made in hell, thus providing more evidence Jack Seward's missionary was correct about the connection between the Japanese language and Satan. The two spoken languages are strikingly different to the ear, as tonal Chinese is literally sung, while Japanese intonation is even flatter than English. Using Chinese writing was even more unfortunate because Chinese is based on ideograms, that is, the characters represent ideas, not sounds as in English. Obviously, there are many more ideas than sounds, which leads to there being approximately 52,000 characters in the language. And you were probably proud when you had learned the 52 upper and lower case characters in the English alphabet!

Karate is a journey,
not a destination.

Electric Babies Say Ten Calculating Looms

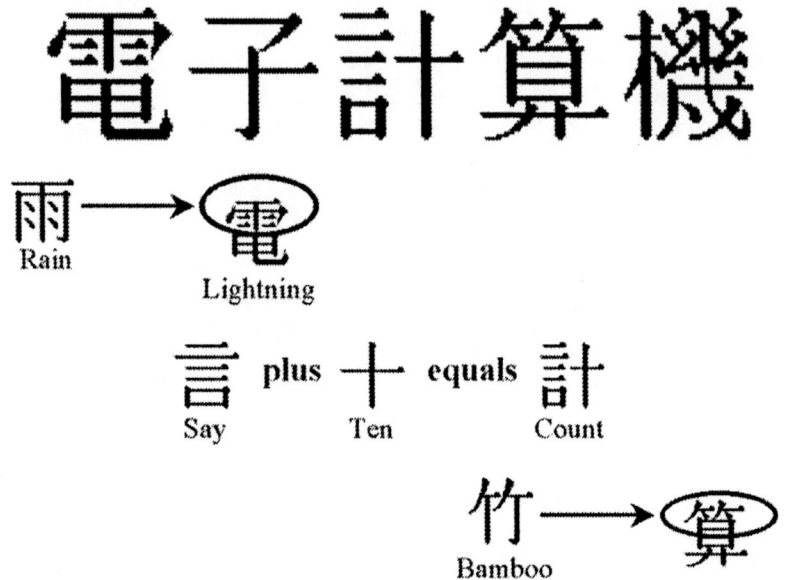

Kanji are ideograms—they stand for ideas, not sounds. Consider the Japanese word shown. I'll tell you that these five characters together represent one English word. Let's see if we can decipher this word. With many Things Japanese it's best to begin at the end. "Things Japanese" is an allusion to Basil Hall Chamberlain's delightful 1905 book *Things Japanese,* which was inexplicably renamed *Japanese Things* by Charles E. Tuttle Company in their 1971 reprint.[25] Tuttle is usually very simpatico with their martial-arts-and-other-Things-Japanese authors, but this is an example of a failure to understand the intent: "Japanese Things" ain't got the ring. Despite Tuttle's rare lapse, it's a great book. But we digress. The last character is a loom. Doesn't it look like a loom to you? If you drink enough saké, lay on the floor, and squint your eyes, it will look unmistakably like a loom to you, too. The loom was about the most sophisticated machine imaginable to the ancient Chinese, so we're looking at a word for some kind of *machine.*

Now that we know where we'll end, let's work from the beginning. The first character is the character for rain, with a little tail hanging out of it. Notice it's coming out of the little cloud. It's lightning, and nowadays stands for *electricity,* since the Confucian sage Ben Franklin told us that lightning was electricity. So we have an *electric machine.*

The second character is the character for *baby*. As you can see, it looks like a little papoose, lending support to the theory American Indians came from Asia. So maybe we have an electric baby machine! Isn't that clever? Instead of having a real baby, you could have this electric baby machine—when you get tired of it, just turn it off and put it on the shelf. But wait, they have plenty of real babies in China, and so an electric baby would be unlikely to have made it past the prototype stage. How about the other way: what's a baby piece of electricity? Why, that would be an electron, wouldn't it? So it's an *electronic machine*.

Now we're getting somewhere. The third character can be divided into two other characters. As with many problems in life, it's necessary to divide and conquer Japanese characters. The left half is a little box with four lines coming out of it. The box is also another character, this one meaning mouth, and the four lines represent sound coming out of the mouth. You might think the character is on its side, since the sound is going up, not out, but apparently even Chinese have to lay on the floor to read characters sometimes. And so that part of the character means *say*. The right half looks like a cross, but since Chinese are mostly Buddhist, it probably isn't supposed to be a cross or grave. Actually, it's the character for the number *ten*. Like the Romans, the Chinese thought a crossed line should mean ten, although the Roman numeral looks like an X. So what could "say tens" mean? How about *count*? You say a lot of tens when you count.

Just one more character to go. Our remaining character shows a *soroban*, or abacus, with a pair of hands at the bottom. Since soroban were originally made from bamboo, the character for bamboo is put at the top as a hint. Then you'll clearly see the soroban (on its side, again) with a pair of hands at the bottom, poised as if over a keyboard. If you can't see that, try a little more saké, you'll see it soon enough. A soroban is a calculator. In fact, at the Japanese national calculating competitions, contestants can choose to use either an electronic calculator or a soroban, but the winner is usually a contestant with a soroban. So this character means *calculate*.

So what do we have? An electronic counting and calculating machine: a *computer*, although most Japanese now call it a kompyutā, which is the closest a Japanese can come to the English word *computer*.

Tachi Kanji

Since the stance is the foundation of all techniques, and our theme for this chapter is grounding, we'll learn the kanji for tachi, or stance. Stances are critical to technique. This character seems to be an easy visual representation for stance, since the kanji itself is so stable looking. It means stand, and thus stance. This is the same tachi that is in the name of the Japanese conglomerate Hitachi, which means literally 'standing in the sun'. It is also combined with kawa, or river, to get Tachikawa, the name of a US Air Force base in Japan.

2.

WATER: Taikyoku Shodan

Strive for a mind that's fluid like water, not rigid. Water will take the shape of the container it's in, be it round or square, adapting itself perfectly to its environment. Water can be a drop to itself, or it can be the entire ocean. Water is clear blue, and I hope to help you achieve the mental clarity needed to be successful in your endeavors.
—Miyamoto Musashi, describing Mizu no Rin, the Ring of Water.

Flowing

There is a saying in Karate, strive for "Mizu no Kokoro"—a Heart and Mind Like Water. "This concept refers to a mind calm and clear like the surface of a pool of water. Such a surface acts as a mirror and reflects all that comes within its range."[26]

If you *try* to remember you will lose.
Empty your mind, be formless, shapeless. Like water.
Now you put water into a cup, it becomes the cup.
You put water into a bottle, it becomes the bottle.
You put water in a teapot, it becomes the teapot.
Now water can flow or creep or drip—or crash!
Be water, my friend.
—Bruce Lee, *The Tao of Gung Fu*[27]

Taikyoku Shodan Choreography

#	Side	Waza	Technique	Tachi	Notes
1	Left	Gedan Barai	Down Block	Zenkutsu	90° Left Turn
2	Right	Oi Zuki	Lunge Punch	Zenkutsu	
3	Right	Gedan Barai	Down Block	Zenkutsu	180° Right Turn
4	Left	Oi Zuki	Lunge Punch	Zenkutsu	
5	Left	Gedan Barai	Down Block	Zenkutsu	90° Left Turn
6	Right	Oi Zuki	Lunge Punch	Zenkutsu	
7	Left	Oi Zuki	Lunge Punch	Zenkutsu	
8	Right	Oi Zuki	Lunge Punch	Zenkutsu	**Kiai!**
9	Left	Gedan Barai	Down Block	Zenkutsu	270° Left Turn
10	Right	Oi Zuki	Lunge Punch	Zenkutsu	
11	Right	Gedan Barai	Down Block	Zenkutsu	180° Right Turn
12	Left	Oi Zuki	Lunge Punch	Zenkutsu	
13	Left	Gedan Barai	Down Block	Zenkutsu	90° Left Turn
14	Right	Oi Zuki	Lunge Punch	Zenkutsu	Heading Home
15	Left	Oi Zuki	Lunge Punch	Zenkutsu	
16	Right	Oi Zuki	Lunge Punch	Zenkutsu	**Kiai!**
17	Left	Gedan Barai	Down Block	Zenkutsu	270° Left Turn
18	Right	Oi Zuki	Lunge Punch	Zenkutsu	
19	Right	Gedan Barai	Down Block	Zenkutsu	180° Right Turn
20	Left	Oi Zuki	Lunge Punch	Zenkutsu	

See the kata performed at www.wadokikai.com.

Taikyoku Shodan Techniques

Zenkutsu Dachi	Front Stance	前屈立ち
Gedan Barai	Down block	下段払い
Oi Zuki	Lunge Punch	追い突き

2. The Flowing Ring of WATER • 27

Shinkokata Number 1

From Gedan Barai (Down Block) Oi Zuki (Lunge Punch) in Zenkutsu Dachi (Front Stance).

Command	Technique	Note
Yōi.	Ready Stance	
Hajime!	Left Gedan Barai	
(Ichi)	Right Oi Zuki	
(Ni)	Left Oi Zuki	
(San)	Right Oi Zuki	
(Shi)	Left Oi Zuki	
(Go)	Right Oi Zuki	Kiai!
Kaesu!	Left Gedan Barai	180° Turn to the Left Counterclockwise
(Ichi)	Right Oi Zuki	
(Ni)	Left Oi Zuki	
(San)	Right Oi Zuki	
(Shi)	Left Oi Zuki	
(Go)	Right Oi Zuki	Kiai!
Yame.	Ready Stance	

Shodan Technique

Taikyoku Shodan is the first kata learned in Wadō Ki Kai. Funakoshi, who invented the kata, had this to say about it:

> Because of its simplicity, the kata is easily learned by beginners. Nevertheless, as its name implies, this form is of the most profound character and one to which, upon mastery of the art of karate, an expert will return to select it as the ultimate training kata.
>
> Once one is able to perform the Taikyoku forms with proficiency, he can understand the other kata with relative ease. For this reason, the Taikyoku form should be considered elementary as well as the ultimate form. In fact, the Taikyoku Kata is the very prototype of a karate kata, a combination of the down block and middle level front punch (basic techniques in any training), the front stance, the typical body movements of karate, and a defined line of movement.[28]

Tadashi Nakamura (b. 1942), 9th Dan, of World Seido Karate Organization, describes it this way: "This foundation kata is common to all styles of karate, and it dates back to the Okinawan practice. It employs one stance throughout (zenkutsu dachi), one basic block (gedan barai) and one basic punch (chudan oizuki). The student is also introduced to the idea of back-turning 180°, to defend against an opponent coming from behind."[29]

The story is told of the founder of Wadō Ki Kai, John T. Pereira, 8th Dan. He was attending a seminar, where each Black Belt was asked to do a kata. The others did many and varied advanced kata, with jumps and whirls and other techniques wondrous to behold. Sensei Pereira, on the other hand, did Taikyoku Shodan, the first kata learned in the WKK System. It would seem a pretty ridiculous kata to do under the circumstances, were it not for the fact his Taikyoku Shodan wowed the audience. He said: "All of this is nothing but that".

Ohshima tells us: "One of his [Master Egami's] favorite practices was to execute the Taikyoku Shodan within fifteen seconds, which is like running all the way."[30] Can you do it in 15 seconds?

Zenkutsu Dachi—Front Stance

Zenkutsu Dachi is the first of the three basic stances we'll learn in Taikyoku. The other two stances, Kōkutsu Dachi and Kiba Dachi, will be introduced in Sandan. Zenkutsu is sometimes written in English as two words Zen Kutsu. Since there are no spaces between words in Japanese, it's a matter of taste which you use; we prefer one word, but two words is perfectly logical, too. The name literally means Front Bending Stance, and is usually called *Front Stance*, or Forward Stance. Zenkutsu appears in all four Taikyoku kata, and is the only stance used in Shodan and Nidan.

The advice Patrick received as a young infantryman going into combat can well be applied to all the stances in Taikyoku, and to most stances in Karate: Stay Low. The natural tendency is to stand too high.

The back foot points off at about 45 degrees.

Training Notes for Zenkutsu

- **Stay Low.** The tendency is to stand too high.
- Even when transitioning from stance to stance or moving forward or back, **don't come up.**
- Remember to keep the **knee over the foot.** If you can see your foot, you're not low enough.
- Stand erect, with the **shoulders up and back**, over the hips, facing forward.
- The back leg should be **straight and locked.**

Gedan Barai—Down Block

Gedan Barai literally means 'Down-Level Sweep'. It can be translated Lower Section Block, Downward Block, or as we usually do, *Down Block*. It is the most common technique in the Taikyoku kata, and the only technique that's in all four kata. It's done in the four kata combined a total of 26 times: 17 on the left and 9 on the right, always with a turn. In fact, most turns use it, although in Sandan, Ude Uke is used for the turns on the wings.

In the Taikyoku kata, Gedan Barai always accompanies a turn. These turns should always be accomplished with a pivoting motion. This is achieved by momentarily perching on the foot, which should be placed so it will define a good stance after the turn. In the 180 degree turns on the wings, for example, the foot actually moves straight across, neither forward nor backward, so your stance will have the same length after the turn as before.

Remember the hand that is not sweeping should protect your groin, *kinteki* in Japanese. Actually, kinteki literally means "Gold Bull's Eye" or "Golden Target". The term is not on any of the major Japanese/English dictionaries, so it's probably fighters' slang. Funakoshi,[31] Sugiyama[32] and others use kinteki for groin. So when attacking, go for the gold, and protect your own golden target at all times!

Don't let your hand sweep past your body. As Musashi says, "Never stop your opponent from doing anything that is useless, but prevent them from doing something that is useful. This is essential to martial arts."[33] If the blow is past your body, it will miss you anyway. You should save the energy and let your opponent waste his.

Training Notes for Gedan Barai

- **Keep Low.**
- Protect your **golden target!** Be sure to **cover your groin** during the preparatory move.
- **Don't lean forward.**
- End with the hand **2 fists** in front of the knee.
- Make sure to start with the **palm to ear.**
- **Don't sweep past** your body.
- Perch & **Pivot!**
- All movement should stop at the **same instant.**

Oi Zuki—Lunge Punch

Oi Tsuki appears in Shodan and Yondan, done a total of 10 times on the right, and 8 on the Left. Oi Zuki is usually translated *Lunge Punch*. The word Tsuki does not literally mean "punch", it means "thrust". This underscores the fact that tsuki need force imparted by the entire body, including especially the hips, not just the arm. The fist, which has the knuckles pointed downward when chambered at the hip, should corkscrew to face upward at the moment of contact. This twist should not be evenly distributed over the course of the punch, but should happen just before contact to impart maximum torque to the target. The fist is in Seiken. Seiken or Sei Ken is usually translated *Regular Fist* but it is literally *Correct Fist*.

☯ ☯ ☯

In the various styles, there is disagreement as to how high the fist should be held when it is waiting to punch—some take the high road and some the low. In WKK, we hold the fist low, on the hip next to the belt, as does Funakoshi.[34] But Nagamine studied under Choki Motobu who he notes positioned his fist high and "posed the knuckle just below the breast and beside the lung."[35] Tae Kwon Do also tends to hold the fist high. Patrick had unconsciously picked up this position. When I first started at WKK, I noticed I automatically chambered the cocked fist high, as high as I could get it. I had never taken Karate, but had apparently picked up the position from schoolyard mimicking. Remember, my schoolyard was in Okinawa. Nagamine notes the high position as different from the lower stance common in Shuri and Tomari, which would explain my tendency, because I lived in Naha for five years. Naha karateka are also noted for lower stances, as is Wadō Ki Kai.

Training Notes for Oi Zuki

- Keep the **fist tight**.
- You'll be sorry if you don't keep your **thumbs in**.
- As always: **Keep Low**. Do the Naha Walk down the center: **marry the knees**.
- **Don't lean forward** to reach the opponent. If you can't reach in a real fight, you're too far away; move in, or kick instead of punch.
- **Delay the twist of the fist** until the last moment before contact.
- All movement should stop at the **same instant**.
- Tense at the moment of impact, then **relax**.

Variations on Shodan

For a showdown on Shodan, we examined four books that detail Taikyoku Shodan: Blot's *Karate: techniques & tactics*, Funakoshi's *Karate-dō Kyōhan: The Master Text*, Nakamura's *Karate: Technique & Spirit*, and Mas Oyama's *Karate School*.[36] All four agree on the moves in Taikyoku Shodan, and are identical with the WKK Taikyoku Shodan.

In addition, some other styles have kata similar to Taikyoku Shodan but with a different name. In Yamaguchi's *Goju-Ryu Karate II*, Taikyoku Gedan has the same techniques in the same order as Wadō Ki Kai's Taikyoku Shodan, although the stance is given as Shiko Dachi at 45 degrees, not Zenkutsu as we use, despite the fact Yamaguchi uses Zenkutsu elsewhere.[37] Shiko Dachi is similar to our Kiba Dachi except the feet point out in the way White Belt's feet tend to accidentally and incorrectly point when they're trying to do Kiba Dachi. Maybe Yamaguchi had the same problem!

In *The Essence of Okinawan Karate-Do*, Nagamine details two Fukyugata, the second of which has similarities with the Wadō Ki Kai Taikyoku Shodan and Nidan. Fukyugata II has two stances, Gedan Barai being delivered low as in WKK, but the other techniques are delivered from a much higher stance, similar to Kamae. The embusen (floor pattern) is the same, but unlike WKK's, where the wings are the same within each kata, the three wings are different from each other. The first wing is like the wing in our Shodan, the second wing is like our Nidan, and the third is like our Shodan again, except the punches are jōdan (upper level) not chūdan (midlevel).

Dojo Lore

Gi

You are required to wear a Karate uniform. It is called a "gi". Sometimes the art is attached, so you might say Karate-gi, to distinguish it from a Judo-gi. Japanese often attach the gi to Dō, meaning Way, but Dogi sounds like "get along little dogie" so we avoid it.

In Wadō Ki Kai, the only additional feature allowed on our gi is the Wadō Ki Kai emblem. Gi color other than white may be worn <u>only</u> by visitors from another dojo. Tie the belt so that you have the appropriate square knot with the ends of the belt even and resting in the center of your body, not at the back or side. Again, visitors from other dojo are exempt from this rule, and should wear their gi appropriately for their style. Never wear a belt color other than the one associated with your rank. Make sure your gi is always clean and ironed (if possible). Cutting off the sleeves or pant legs is not permitted. If your gi begins to look tattered, buy a new one. It is a reflection of you and your school.

Japanese undertakers cross the gi right over left on cadavers, so always place the left side of your gi over the right side, unless you're dead. If you're hopelessly outmatched in a sparring contest you might decide to cross right over left to save the mortuary some trouble.

Shodan Kanji

Dan

The several Taikyoku kata are named for their dan (pronounced like the name "Don", not "Dan"). Appropriately enough, the left half of the kanji for dan has what looks like steps (if you squint your eyes and turn your head sideways). Dan means *level*, and is also used to denote black belt degrees. From two up, degrees are assigned numbers: nidan is composed of ni, or two, plus dan; sandan is san, three, plus dan; yondan is four plus dan.

The first kata is called Shodan, as is the first Black Belt degree. The *sho* of Shodan is actually written with the kanji that means 'begin'. Japanese characters are called kanji, and denote an idea, not a sound, so can be pronounced completely differently depending on the context, as long as the meaning is the same. This kanji for beginner can also be pronounced 'haji', as in "Hajime!", the command to begin an exercise. Apparently it is too cruel to tell karateka who worked hard for four or five years to finally attain black belt that they have actually only reached Beginning Level, so it is usually translated 'First Degree' when referring to belts. The table shows your path, all the way to 10th Degree. As an added bonus, the table also shows you how the numerals are written in Japanese and Chinese, with the exception of one, which looks like two, except with only one line. Note kyu count down, dan up. A 2nd Kyu outranks a 3rd kyu, but a 3rd Dan outranks a 2nd Kyu.

If you keep doing what you've been doing,

You'll keep getting what you've been getting.

RANK

Shodan	初段	Beginner
Nidan	二段	2nd Degree
Sandan	三段	3rd Degree
Yondan	四段	4th Degree
Godan	五段	5th Degree
Rokudan	六段	6th Degree
Nanadan	七段	7th Degree
Hachidan	八段	8th Degree
Kudan	九段	9th Degree
Judan	十段	10th Degree

TECHNIQUE LEVEL

Jodan	上段	Upper Level, Upward
Chudan	中段	Midlevel
Gedan	下段	Lower Level, Downward

Gedan Barai uses the same dan, meaning level, that we see in shodan and nidan. This time it's combined with the word that means down or lower, thus down-level. You'll notice this kanji looks like a T for "Take that!" with a little arm pointing down in the kanji, just like the sweeping arm in this technique. As with the word level in English, dan can, in addition to meaning level as in level of accomplishment, also mean level as in how high. This meaning of dan is usually combined with Jo, Ge, or Chu—Up, Down or Middle—to signify the height of the technique. For a kick, for example, a gedan technique might aim at the knee, chudan at the midsection or chest, and jodan the chin. Note Jodan is Gedan flipped over, but gravity pulled the arm down.

Belts and Ranks

Dan is also used for belts, namely the degree of Black Belt. Below black belts, the colored belts are ranked as kyu, which count down, not up. Thus 8th dan is a very high black belt and an 8th kyu a very low colored belt.

To begin with, each student should realize that a belt is merely a symbol of one's knowledge and experience. A belt does not mean that one person's worth is any different from another's. People progress at different rates. Some learn faster than others, some have more time to invest, some are physically or mentally more adept at katas (forms), while others seem more skillful at kumite (sparring). The objective of this program is not to see how high a rank you can achieve, but how much knowledge you can gain. A beginner could go to a store and buy a black belt and put it around their waist. Would this individual have the knowledge of a person who had earned the rank of black belt? Certainly not. At the other end of the spectrum, a person with 40 years of experience could put a white belt around their waist. Would they lose the 40 years of knowledge they had attained simply by putting on a lower ranking belt? Indeed, not. Again, a belt is only a symbol. As John Pereira said in his poem *Technique*: "The person whose verdict counts most in your life is the one staring back from the glass."

A colored belt not only carries a rank with it but also responsibilities. These duties involve teaching, being an exemplary model for lower ranking students, and being a wholesome representative of the dojo. The details of these responsibilities will be explained to you as your rank gets higher.

Counting Dan & Kyū

As in English, numbers are idiosyncratic in Japanese. In English, four and fourteen have a U, forty doesn't. Three becomes thir- in thirteen and thirty. Eleven and twelve, first and second have special names. Likewise in Japanese, counting has its oddities, so you'll just have to memorize the names.

#	Dan	Kyū
1	Shodan	Ikkyū
2	Nidan	Nikyū
3	Sandan	Sankyū
4	Yondan or Yodan	Yonkyū
5	Godan	Gokyū
6	Rokudan	Rokkyū
7	Nanadan or Shichidan	Shichikyū
8	Hachidan	Hachikyū
9	Kudan	Kyukyū
10	Jūdan	

Testing Time

In our school system, promotionals are held every six months. Testing can be done at any of our schools.

Test Criteria

Strength is a fundamental criterion when testing, and is based primarily on the training level a person is at. The techniques, movements, power, and force a student exhibits should be commensurate with a student's experience and rank. This is the immediate concern of the actual test. One is also measured by personal growth. Development of impulse control, humaneness toward others, etc. are closely examined. These attributes are on-going concerns throughout martial arts training, and hopefully, throughout our lives.

Judging

The judgment as to whether the student meets the minimum standards of performance for his/her prospective rank is made by a group of judges. The judges consist of experienced black belts from the different schools of the Wadō Ki Kai system, and occasionally, from other instructors (Black Belts) from different Karate styles. The judges meet periodically throughout the year to discuss a variety of topics concerning the martial arts, but also to examine the progression of their students in achieving the goals defined for each semester.

Rationale

Emotionally, we respond to real life self-defense situations in much the same way as we respond to test taking. By putting our bodies through the correct Karate movements and techniques during formal examinations, we are better preparing ourselves for real life situations. Karateka who have survived both life-threatening attacks and the rigors of martial art examinations will tell you that they have experienced few emotional differences between the two; fear, anxiety, anger, etc. We therefore value formal testing as a way of learning to direct these emotions into proper and practiced defense.

With our program, the ranking system, showing what the karateka studies at each level, is as shown in the table.

9. WHITE Belt	Taikyoku (Shodan, Nidan, Sandan and Yodan). Just Starting.
8. YELLOW Belt	Pingan (Shodan, Nidan, and Sandan). Kumite. Minimum of 6 months.
7. ORANGE Belt	Pingan (Yodan and Godan), Nahanchi. Kumite. Minimum of 1 year.
6. GREEN Belt	Jion and Saifa. Kumite. Minimum of 1½ years.
5. BLUE Belt	Potsai Dai and Chinto. Kumite. Minimum of 2 years.
4. PURPLE Belt	Unsa, Empi and Seisan. Kumite. Minimum of 2½ years.
3. BROWN Belt 3rd Kyu	Sushi no Sho and Sakugawa no Sho (Bo). Kumite. Minimum of 3 years.
2. BROWN Belt 2nd Kyu	Gay Pa, Soea and Giokerin (Sai). Kumite. Minimum of 3½ years.
1. BROWN Belt 1st Kyu	Kusanku Shō. Kumite. Minimum of 4 years.
1. BLACK Belt 1st Dan	Matsumura-Potsai, Matsumura-Jion, Nijushiho, and Kusanku-Dai. Minimum of 4½ years.
2. BLACK Belt 2nd Dan	Unsu, Useishi, and Seinchin. Minimum of 5½ years.
3. BLACK Belt 3rd Dan	One year of teaching. Minimum of 7½ years.

At each level, the student is responsible for *all* the techniques of previous levels, and is expected to show improvement and refinement in each.

Students trying out for any degree of Black Belt must show strong fighting ability and execute at least ippon (one point) in each kumite match. In most styles, degrees of Black Belt beyond Sandan are granted on the basis of contributions to the Art, through teaching, writing, research, or innovation.

These are the requirements as they stand today. As knowledge is gained, we may add to these requirements. We note this in the spirit of understanding that no system reaches perfection, and to live, we must change and adapt.

Rank and corresponding belt colors are achieved on the basis of performance examinations in the areas of kata, shinkokata, kumite, and bunkai-oyo. Each level of kata is associated with a particular set of shinkokata, kumite, and bunkai-oyo. As students advance through the ranks, they are expected to become more proficient and have a greater understanding of what they are doing.

Bunkai

Bunkai-oyo refers to the analysis of kata moves and their self-defense applications. It is the traditional way of practicing Karate. At our school, we practice bunkai-oyo on a regular basis so that students understand what they are doing and why. However, the first test that includes this as a component of an examination is First-Degree Black Belt. The candidate will be asked to explain and demonstrate with a partner(s), the application of some of the moves of any given kata.

Many people practice a kata without knowing the bunkai. In fact, there is often disagreement over what the bunkai actually is, with several plausible interpretations. You might have had the experience of one Black Belt telling you a certain technique is used for one purpose, and another telling you it is for a completely different purpose. At first you probably thought one or both of them had sparred too often without adequate head protection. But surprisingly, they were probably both right. This might seem confusing, but actually it's a good thing and is a result of the fact that any one technique can serve you in several ways.

Consider **Ushiro Hiji Uchi**, the *Rear Elbow Strike*. Interestingly, it's another bunkai for the punch. When punching, the retreating hand should always be pulled back with some force, and thought of as giving momentum to the striking hand. If an attacker has grabbed you from behind, the elbow of the retreating hand can actually be an attack to the rear. Thinking of the retreating arm as an elbow strike to someone behind you will also improve your punch to the front since the momentum to the rear will turn your body and increase the forward thrust to the punching hand. There are two Japanese words that you'll hear around the dojo, bunkai and oyo, in relation to a technique's application, and whose use in English has some controversy.

Bunkai & Oyo Controversy

Bunkai means *analysis* or *resolution*, while **ōyō** means *application*, or as a verb *put to practical use.* The controversy arises over whether the word *bunkai* as used by American karateka should be more properly replaced with *oyo.* Some argue bunkai is the explanation of how to do the move, not its use, but most Americans use the term to mean application, as in "The bunkai of this technique is to kick your opponent's testicles up into his throat". Perhaps there is a special meaning for bunkai in Japanese dojo, but it seems the word bunkai in MSJ (Modern Standard Japanese) would be acceptable the way Americans use it. It is written with the same character for analysis that appears in the job title Systems Analyst, a title Patrick held for some years. As with the controversy over the analysis of bunkai versus application of oyo, some systems analysts argue: "Analysis does not include design. You must never let design enter your mind during analysis." This is profoundly silly. Imagine someone telling you he has just completed a thorough analysis of a vehicle:

"What kind of vehicle?" you ask him.

"I don't know, that's a design issue and I *analyzed* the vehicle", he replies.

So you ask: "Well, what will it be used for?"

"I have no idea, that's a design question and I was doing analysis", he replies.

You probe further: "Does it roll, or fly, or float?"

"Beats me, that's application and I did an analysis", he replies.

Etc., etc., etc.

This obviously makes no sense: you can't analyze something if you don't even know what it's used for, and this would apply to Karate techniques as well. So the American use of bunkai would be acceptable in Japanese, and even if not, the word has entered the English language of karateka meaning "the purpose of a technique". Thus as our vehicle might serve several uses, a Karate technique can have several bunkai. The technique with the most bunkai might well be Gedan Barai, so let's look at it in more detail.

75 Gedan Barai

There are many bunkai for Gedan Barai. It is traditionally described as a block of a low kick, and sometimes called Gedan Barai Uke, *uke* meaning *block*, to emphasize the blocking. Perhaps the uke is usually dropped for a reason, namely that Gedan Barai can be used for many things other than a block. Sensei Arce once saw a demo of over one hundred uses for this technique. There is a book by Rick Clark called *75 Down Blocks* that illustrates there are many possibilities other than a block. In fact, Clark limits himself to "only 75" interpretations, implying there are more, in this excerpt:[38]

> Because this book was designed to cover only seventy-five techniques, there are limitations to the number of attacks discussed. Each chapter contains bunkai for the down block in four to eight scenarios. They include:
>
>   1. Defense against a kick
>   2. Defense against a same-side wrist grab
>   3. Defense against a cross-hand wrist grab
>   4. Defense against a double-wrist grab
>   5. Defense against an upper-arm grab
>   6. Preemptive techniques
>   7. Defense against a push
>   8. Defense against a single-hand lapel grab
>   9. Defense against a double-hand grab to the upper body
> 10. Defense against a grab from the rear
> 11. Defense against a punch
> 12. Defense against a stick"

Notice category 6 is Preemptive Techniques, which by definition are not blocks, but attacks. They are clearly offensive, not defensive. Clark does include many blocks, but also strikes with the fist, and elbow strikes to the neck. As in the West, where the combative arts have been divided into wrestling and boxing, in Japan they were divided into Jūdō and Karate, with grappling in Judo and striking in Karate. But Clark includes arm bars and locks; and even leg bars. This would make sense in street fighting since in many barroom brawls the participants end up grappling on the floor.

Shodan Philosophy

Ken Zen Itchi

拳禅一致

Zen is closely related to Karate, at least in legend. There is even a saying, Ken Zen Itchi, "The Fist and Zen are One". It appears the Chinese Martial Arts have their roots at the Shaolin Temple in China, where they were introduced, sometime around 520 c.e., by a monk named Bodhidarma. He is called Daruma in Japanese, and is shown here in a portrait by Miyamoto Musashi. According to legend, Daruma also introduced Zen to the Shaolin Temple. In fact, it's said Daruma introduced Kung Fu for physical fitness. Long periods of meditation led

to poor physical condition, which in turn affected meditation. If true, martial arts were originally an aid to meditation, rather than the other way around.

There is some dispute over how much of Karate can be traced to China and how much is native Okinawan, but suffice it to say there is an unmistakable Chinese influence. In Oakland Chinatown there is a building on the corner of Webster and 13th Streets that has a large sign proclaiming "Shaolin Kung Fu" in English.* Shaolin is written with the very same characters that are pronounced Shōrin in Japanese, and is the name of a prominent style of Okinawan Karate, thus making the connection apparent. Shorin styles are sometimes even called Shorin Ji, which means Shaolin Temple, making the Chinese connection even more obvious. Shorin was an influence on WKK, both directly, and through Shorin's influence on Shotokan, which strongly influenced Wadō Ki Kai.

Proponents of the Chinese Martial Arts are quick to criticize Okinawans as historically inaccurate, and even ungrateful, for not acknowledging the Chinese connection at every opportunity. When discussing their Martial Arts, Okinawans downplay Chinese influence based on the fact the stories are legends, the truth hidden in the mist of time. And besides, they say, any legacy was significantly

---

* In Chinese Characters, incidentally, it says *Shaolin Gate*, not *Shaolin Kung Fu*.

adapted by the Okinawans, thus making it their own. But it turns out Daruma came to China from *India*, bringing his arts from there. When discussing their martial arts, Chinese downplay Indian influence based on the fact the stories are legends, the truth hidden in the mist of time. And besides, they say, any legacy was significantly adapted by the Chinese, thus making it their own.

Many martial artists, including the Samurai of olde, have found Zen essential to the Art. Many books on martial arts include Zen in the title, including:

C.W. Nicol's *Moving Zen*
Nathan J. Johnson's *Barefoot Zen*
Randall Hassell's *Zen Pen & Sword: The Karate Experience*
Chuck Norris' *The Secret Power Within: Zen Solutions to Real Problems*
Deshimaru Taisen's *The Zen Way to the Martial Arts*
Joe Hyams's *Zen in the Martial Arts*
Mark Bishop's *Zen Kobudo*
Winston I. King's *Zen & the Way of the Sword* and first, so not least
Eugen Herrigel's *Zen in the Art of Archery*

Some karateka do not have the patience, or inclination, for long periods of zazen, or seated meditation. Patrick notes: "The mokusō at the beginning and end of Karate class is near my limit. I find this ritual both pleasant and helpful, but have no interest in a program like some Aikido dojo, where as many hours are devoted to meditation as to Aikidō itself." C.W. Nicol's book refers to kata in the title as *Moving Zen*. He got the title from something Takagi Sensei, the then Director of the Japan Karate Association, told him: "If you practice hard you will develop a mind that is as calm as still water. Karate is moving Zen, and Zen is the state that you must strive for." Nicol goes on to say "Through concentration on perfection the mind is released, and a great calm, in which the body moves, is achieved. Practice of kata was the best way to know the Zen calm."[39] Incidentally, we have a Karate book written in Japanese that has a red banner ("obi") around it with an endorsement of the book by Nicol. A book on Karate written in Japanese by a Japanese for Japanese has a Japanese publisher who sought approval from a Westerner![40] Good job, C.W.!

Grant Butterfield, Sensei at the Bladium in Alameda, relates how on a grueling long-distance run he completely lost awareness while mentally performing kata. Patrick: "Although I've yet to attain it fully or consistently, this is the kind of Zen

I can appreciate, the Zen of concentration, the Zen of doing, the Zen of kata—Moving Zen."

Nihongo

Karate Kanji

You should learn to read the name of our Martial Art. Karate (Please! NOT "cuh ROT tee", but "kah rah tay") is written with two kanji, kara, "empty", and te, "hand".

Kara

Let's look at the kanji that make the word Karate. The first character, kara, has a very complex set of meanings, and was once, and to some extent still is, the center of some controversy. Suffice it to say that the kanji used for kara was once a different kanji, one that evoked the Chinese roots of the art. The old character means Tang (no, not the breakfast drink), as in the Tang Dynasty 618-907, and is used poetically to mean China. There were implications that the change had an element of racism (or more correctly nationalism, or ethnic superiority, since under most definitions, the Chinese and Japanese are of the same race), since it was made in the 1930s at a time when Japan was involved in a dirty little war with China.

Karate	空手	Our Art
Todi	唐手	Chinese Hand
Harai	払	Sweep
Ken	拳	Fist
Kempo	拳法	Law of the Fist
Oi Zuki	追突	Lunge Punch

The Tang character can also be pronounced Tō in Japanese, that being the closest Japanese can get to Tang, so Tote is sometimes used to mean Karate written the old way, since the Kara of Karate cannot be pronounced To. Masters Publication did this in their re-print of Funakoshi's 1922 book, since Funakoshi used the Tang character in that book's title.[41] In Hogen the Te becomes Di, so it is sometimes pronounced Tōdi in Okinawa.

The fact it was possible to change kanji without changing the pronunciation of the word illustrates the difference between the English and Japanese writing systems. In Japanese, the kanji characters denote meanings, not sounds. So two characters with different meanings can be pronounced the same, and a character can be pronounced differently at different times. For example, the kanji kara can be pronounced (take a deep breath): Kū, Sora, Su, Kara, A, Muna, Utsu, or Utsuke. That number of pronunciations, usually called readings, is above average, but not unique—most kanji have two or three readings, but some have a dozen.

Japan's culture was profoundly affected by China, much as English culture was affected by Greece and Rome. This is reflected in the language: there are as many words of Chinese origin in Japanese as there are Latin words in English. So the typical kanji will have two readings: one based on the Chinese pronunciation of the word, and the other will be the native Japanese word that corresponds to that Chinese word. The languages are very different, however, so words of Chinese origin will not be recognizable to a Chinese once they've gone into Japanese. At the time the Japanese were importing Chinese words, for example, there was apparently a tragedy at sea, and the ship with all the Ls on it was lost with all its cargo. Consequently, Ls had to become Rs: Shaolin became Shorin.

Kara is usually translated as "empty", but the character actually has some complex connotations. Japan's gift(?) to world entertainment, karaoke, uses the very same kara. The oke part is short for the English word orchestra, and is written with the katakana syllabary that is used to transliterate foreign words into Japanese, instead of kanji. So the idea is you can sing with an empty, or nonexistent, orchestra. And often with empty, or nonexistent, singing ability, for that matter.

Kara can be divided into two pieces, top and bottom. This brings us a strategy for remembering kanji. Divide and conquer: you can usually break a complex character into two or even three or four components, or parts. Some of the components appear again and again, and some (214 in fact) have been recognized as *radicals*, and given their own name. Kanji dictionaries are usually arranged by radical, which is unfortunate, because radicals present problems even for the native Japanese, and are extremely problematical to the gaijin (as foreigners are called in Japan). Sometimes the pieces are kanji in themselves, and that is true in this case. The top character means hole or cave, and the bottom means construction. The top half, hole, can be further subdivided into two pieces, which also are radicals. The top half that looks like a little roof (a flat roof, with a decoration on top) is a radical, as are the two little legs holding it up. So the problem: which of those four radicals—cave, construction, roof or legs—should you look under to find it in the dictionary? The rule is it will be classified under the radical most related to its meaning. Yeah, but if you knew the meaning, you wouldn't be looking it up, would you?

So, to summarize the confusion about kanji components. Some kanji are used as components in other kanji. Some of them are officially designated as radicals, with all the rights and benefits that entails. But sometimes a kanji had a poor agent, and somehow did not get to be a radical, despite the fact it sure looks like it ought to be, and appears as a component in many other kanji. Some radicals even have another radical within them, and steal kanji from the smaller radical. And some radicals with good marketing skills aren't even kanji at all, and can only appear as part of another kanji. What else can we say, life ain't fair, even for kanji! As it happens, the radical sometimes depends on which dictionary you are using. Spahn & Hadamitzky, often referred to as S&H, list Kara under the roof, what they call radical 3m.[42] Nelson puts it in the cave, historical radical number 116.[43]

Ignore the roof and hole mnemonics for this character, since the compounds are obvious to any karateka. The top half is no cave: it's a little karateka: a practitioner of Karate! Looks like he's doing a jump kick, or maybe it's a female karateka, and she's doing that kneeling punch at the beginning of Kata Empi. That's not a roof, it's her arms, and her head, bent over.

The bottom half is the embusen, or pattern marked out on the floor, of the kata she's performing. Many kata, especially the basics—Taikyoku, Pingan or Heian 1 and 2, etc., trace a pattern on the floor that looks like the Roman numeral I. What character do the Japanese use to describe this pattern? You remember, the character kō, the very same kanji that forms the bottom half of this character! So your mnemonic: Karateka does kata I. Feel free to think of the I as a roman numeral I, the letter I, or best yet, the Japanese Kō Embusen. So the mnemonic, or trick for remembering this kanji, is "Karateka is practicing her kata". We'll see her again when we talk about tsuki, or punch.

The character doesn't just mean empty, it also has some mystical connotations. It can mean "The Void". What's The Void? It's the all and the nothing. The void is nothing, the void is everything. All things came from the void, and will return to it. The void is within every thing, and everything is within the void. That doesn't make a lot of sense to us, either, but hey, we told you it would be mystical. "The Void" is also the title of Chapter 5, so we'll talk more about it there, but to fully understand this and other mysteries you'll just have to look for our next book.

Te

The second kanji in Karate is te. This one is supposed to look like a hand. Okay, you may have to drink some more saké. Te was once the name for what we call Karate. Patrick McCarthy has translated the minutes of a 1936 meeting at which the change of the name to Karate was discussed. Several attendees noted the art had previously often been called just Te, including Chojun Miyagi: "Most people who come to my place wanting to learn usually just ask if I can teach them te."[44] Japanese characters can change their pronunciation as long as they maintain their meaning. We do this to a limited extent in English, as for example the characters 1 & 2 are pronounced "fur" and "secka" when they are written 1st & 2nd. Te can also be pronounced shu, as in shutō, the sword hand, which we'll see in Taikyoku Sandan. Te is used as a radical or component of many kanji. We'll see it in different guises demonstrating transformation in kanji like ken and harai.

Ken

The **ken** of Seiken means *fist*. You'll notice the kanji for Te appears within the kanji for ken, at the bottom. This is very common: one kanji will appear in a more complex kanji, to give a hint about its meaning (Or sometimes to lead you astray). With the shift of N to M (since it's followed by P) ken is also the kem of Kempō. The second kanji in Kempo means method, law, principle or system, so Kempo means literally *The Law of The Fist*, and at one point, like Te, bid fair to be the name for what we call Karate. Funakoshi actually named his first book *Ryūkyū Kempō* in 1922, Ryukyu being the name of the archipelago whose main island is Okinawa, and Choki Motobu called his 1926 book *Okinawan Kempō*. The characters for Kempo are pronounced Gung Fu or Kung Fu in Cantonese, Chuan Fa in Mandarin.[*] Karate is derived from a centuries-old Okinawan art of

---

[*] *Mandarin* is believed by the communist government of the PRC to be too reminiscent of the Mandarin ruling class, so the dialect is often referred to as Beijing Dialect. It's also sometimes called Pekinese, which sounds too much like a certain small, furry animal for our taste.

self-defense that was itself influenced by Chinese Kempo. The Kempo/Kung Fu identity is another piece of evidence suggesting Chinese influence on the Okinawan Martial Arts. The term Kempo today is applied to certain styles of Karate. Patrick overheard conversations in Okinawa like the following: "I'm studying Shorin Ryu. What style of Karate are you taking?" Answer: "I'm taking Kempo." Attaching the kanji ken to the name of the Taikyoku kata gives 'Taikyoku Ken', which is what the Japanese call the venerable and majestic art that in English, and Chinese, is called Tai Chi.

Harai

The word **harai** (the H became B in the combination Gedan Barai by phonetic shift) actually means *sweep*, not block. The character Te appears in this kanji, too, this time on the left. Notice it's been simplified to the three-stroke radical called tehen, to make it easier to write. This is another example of deviltry, often the character meant to help you is transformed so you won't even recognize it. Originally Harai meant to sweep away something with hand, so the left half of the character is meant to be a stylized hand, and the right half looks like an elbow bent in preparation for the sweep. But now the character means sweep away any way. For example, in Jūdō, the Deashi Barai is the Foot Sweep, and in Kendō, Harai Waza are techniques for warding off your opponent's sword by sweeping with your own. Don't forget to pronounce the Ai like Eliza Doolittle would. "The rine in spine sties minely in the pline" not "The rain in Spain stays mainly in the plain",[45] so it's close "Buh Rye" not "Buh Ray". In fact, Eliza pronounced most of her vowels correctly for Japanese, so if you can imitate her, you'll do fine.

Oi Zuki

Oi Zuki, also written Oi Dzuki, is usually translated *Lunge Punch*. **Oi**, however, literally means *chase*, so it is also translated *Chasing Punch*. The character further means drive away, follow, and pursue. The enclosure to the left and bottom in the kanji is the widespread radical for movement, and Henshall in his *Guide to Remembering Japanese Characters* suggests you think of the two boxes as buttocks, the mnemonic being a butt surrounded by movement, as in chase his butt,[46] a useful visualization, perhaps.

The kanji **Tsuki**, which is how the kanji for Zuki is pronounced when it stands alone apart from a compound, revisits our little friend, the Karateka, from Kara.

This time she's above the character for big, which is a man with his arms spread wide, perhaps telling a story of the big fish he almost caught. But this time, he's actually flat on his back with his arms and legs spread. Our karateka learned her kata well, and has punched out the big bad man. Our brave karateka kneels over him, with steely determination to strike again if he attempts to rise, proud but not arrogant. The mnemonic: Karateka punches big bad guy.

Consonant Shifts

The Zuki of Oi Zuki is a variation of the word Tsuki. The Dachi of Zenkutsu Dachi is a variation of the word Tachi. These are both examples of consonant shifts. **Tachi** is a word by itself meaning *stance*, but can be combined with other words to make the name of a stance. For example, the Front Stance is Zenkutsu Dachi. In English you can, as we usually do, capitalize the name as a proper noun, Front Stance, or even hyphenate it Front-stance. Eventually it could theoretically become a compound word, Frontstance. In Japanese, when a word is attached to another word to form a compound or name, there is often a phonetic shift in the consonant to emphasize the combination. There are several common shifts. The one we see here is from a T to a D. Although the word for stance is tachi, spelt with a T, in combination it becomes dachi with a D. So the Horse Stance we'll learn in Sandan is Kiba Dachi, not Kiba Tachi. Actually, Kiba Tachi would be perfectly understandable, but it would sound better as Kiba Dachi, and would emphasize the fact these two words should be thought of as forming a single concept. Kiba tachi might be more appropriate if you were talking about the stance of a real live horse, so be careful whose stance you call Kiba Tachi.

Actually, the shift is not as much as you might think. In Japanese, the D is considered a variation on the T, rather than a separate letter. For example, if you asked a Japanese to put Ta, Da, Te, De, To, and Do in alphabetical order, he'd look at you puzzled, because to a Japanese, they are already *in* alphabetical order. Ts and Ds are mixed together in Japanese dictionaries, and in written kanji, you can't tell whether the writer pronounced the word with T or D. When written in kana, T and D use the same character; to get Da, for example, you can put two dots next to Ta, as shown in this table of the phonetic shifts we'll encounter in Taikyoku.

The table below shows the phonetic shifts we will encounter in the Taikyoku Kata. Note you will find the word in a Japanese-English dictionary in the original form: you will not find geri in the dictionary, you must look under keri. In a dictionary in Japanese alphabetical order, it's of course not a problem since keri and geri alphabetize to the same spot.

H BECOMES B

は ha ==> ば ba

K BECOMES G

け ke ==> げ ge

N BECOMES M

ん n ==> ん m

(same in Japanese)

T BECOMES D

た ta ==> だ da

Ts BECOMES Z (Dz)

つ tsu ==> づ zu (dzu)

Word	Shifted	Meaning	Examples	Meaning
Harai	Barai	Sweep	Gedan Barai, Ashi Barai	Down Block, Foot Sweep
Keri	Geri	Kick	Mae Geri, Mawashi Geri	Front Kick, Roundhouse Kick
Tachi	Dachi	Stance	Kiba Dachi, Zenkutsu Dachi	Horse Stance, Front Stance
Tsuki	Zuki	Punch	Oi Zuki, Gyaku Zuki	Lunge Punch, Reverse Punch

Zen

The first character of Zenkutsu, **zen**, means *front*, and should not be confused with the Zen of meditation. Japan unfortunately took its writing system from China. We say "unfortunately", because Chinese would have the most compli-cated writing system in the world, except for the fact the Japanese have taken the Chinese system and made it even more complicated, and so easily claim the honor(?) of being the most complicated. Taking Chinese into Japanese was prob-lematical since the two languages are quite different. Chinese is a tonal language, and has a singsong quality to it. Japanese, on the other hand, is monotonal. Two Chinese words can be spelled the same in Japanese (or English for that matter, since English isn't tonal, either) but would sound quite different in Chinese because they would be sung at a different tone. If you're curious about other Asian languages, Vietnamese is tonal like Chinese; Korean, like Japanese and English, is not. Japanese does not allow consonants to fall at the end of a syllable, so these consonants are usually lost when the Chinese word comes into Japanese. This means that several different words in Chinese will become the same word in Japanese. And the Chinese words came into Japanese at different times, and from different Chinese dialects, transliterated by different people, so the Chinese word might have been transliterated several ways. And the Japanese, or the Chinese, might have already had two words for the same idea. Add to that the fact Japanese has fewer possible syllables than most other languages. All these factors mean there are usually at least two readings for the same character, and sometimes many more, so you're left with the following bewildering array of characters, all of which can be read "Zen" (The first kanji is the Zen of meditation, the second is the zen of Zenkutsu):

全占栓煽舛遷僣

然先撰煎腺選亘

漸仙扇潛羨踐苫

善蟬戰染纖賤揃

千釧川洗線賤鮮

蟬喘尖淺箭詮閃

前膳專泉穿薦銑

禪繕宣梅旋船錢

3.

FIRE: Taikyoku Nidan

"Because the situation is one of an instant, the Fire Chapter deals with daily training, considering each moment as a decisive one, and not letting the mind go slack." [47]
—Miyamoto Musashi, describing Hi no Rin, the Ring of Fire.

Fighting

Okinawa was the site of one of the most horrific battles in the history of the world. On April 1, 1945, an Easter Sunday and April Fool's Day, ironically called "Love Day" by the attacking forces, a savage battle began quietly, as General Ushijima decided to play a mind-game, and not oppose the landing on the beautiful sun-drenched beaches of Higashi. From the peaceful landing sprung a fierce campaign, in which the 29th Regiment, USMC, for example, suffered the greatest losses suffered by any US Marine Regiment in a single battle ever, before or since. Both Commanding Generals, Mitsuru Ushijima on the Japanese side and Simon Buckner on the American, died during the battle. By many measures, the Battle of Okinawa saw the greatest loss of naval tonnage of any battle in world history. The battle was also characterized by the widespread use of the Kamikaze, as approximately 5,000 young Japanese on suicide missions died succeeding or attempting to fly their airplanes directly into their targets.

Okinawa was devastated, approximately one-third of its civilian population killed, including many accomplished karateka. In a supreme testament to the folly of war, following the war many American soldiers learned the art of Karate from the survivors, which is an important factor in Karate's worldwide prominence today.

Taikyoku Nidan Choreography

#	Side	Waza	Technique	Tachi	Notes
1	Left	Gedan Barai	Down Block	Zenkutsu	90° Left Turn
2	Right	Age Uke	Rising Block	Zenkutsu	
3	Right	Gedan Barai	Down Block	Zenkutsu	180° Right Turn
4	Left	Age Uke	Rising Block	Zenkutsu	
5a	Left	Gedan Barai	Down Block	Zenkutsu	90° Left Turn
5b	Right	Gyaku Zuki	Reverse Punch	Zenkutsu	
6a	Right	Mae Geri	Front Kick	Zenkutsu	
6b	Left	Gyaku Zuki	Reverse Punch	Zenkutsu	
7a	Left	Mae Geri	Front Kick	Zenkutsu	
7b	Right	Gyaku Zuki	Reverse Punch	Zenkutsu	
8a	Right	Mae Geri	Front Kick	Zenkutsu	
8b	Left	Gyaku Zuki	Reverse Punch	Zenkutsu	**Kiai!**
9	Left	Gedan Barai	Down Block	Zenkutsu	270° Left Turn
10	Right	Age Uke	Rising Block	Zenkutsu	
11	Right	Gedan Barai	Down Block	Zenkutsu	180° Right Turn
12	Left	Age Uke	Rising Block	Zenkutsu	
13a	Left	Gedan Barai	Down Block	Zenkutsu	90° Left Turn
13b	Right	Gyaku Zuki	Reverse Punch	Zenkutsu	
14a	Right	Mae Geri	Front Kick	Zenkutsu	Heading Home
14b	Left	Gyaku Zuki	Reverse Punch	Zenkutsu	
15a	Left	Mae Geri	Front Kick	Zenkutsu	
15b	Right	Gyaku Zuki	Reverse Punch	Zenkutsu	
16a	Right	Mae Geri	Front Kick	Zenkutsu	
16b	Left	Gyaku Zuki	Reverse Punch	Zenkutsu	**Kiai!**
17	Left	Gedan Barai	Down Block	Zenkutsu	270° Left Turn
18	Right	Age Uke	Rising Block	Zenkutsu	
19	Right	Gedan Barai	Down Block	Zenkutsu	180° Right Turn
20	Left	Age Uke	Rising Block	Zenkutsu	

See the kata performed at www.wadokikai.com.

Taikyoku Nidan Techniques

Age Uke	揚げ受け	Rising Block
Gedan Barai	下段払い	Down Block
Gyaku Zuki	逆突き	Reverse Punch
Mae Geri	前蹴り	Front Kick
Zenkutsu Dachi	前屈立ち	Front Stance

Shinkokata Number 2

From Gedan Barai (Down Block) Age Uke (Rising Block) in Zenkutsu Dachi (Front Stance).

Command	Technique	Note
Yōi.	Ready Stance	
Hajime!	Left Gedan Barai	
(Ichi)	Right Age Uke	
(Ni)	Left Age Uke	
(San)	Right Age Uke	
(Shi)	Left Age Uke	
(Go)	Right Age Uke	Kiai!
Kaesu!	Left Gedan Barai	180° Turn to the Left Counterclockwise
(Ichi)	Right Age Uke	
(Ni)	Left Age Uke	
(San)	Right Age Uke	
(Shi)	Left Age Uke	
(Go)	Right Age Uke	Kiai!
Yame.	Ready Stance	

Nidan Technique

Nidan is not to be confused with No Dan, which is what you get when you get confused. In Nidan, we encounter our first combination, the Taikyoku's only kicking technique, and an upper-level block to go with Gedan Barai.

Age Uke—Rising Block

Age literally means hoist, so **Age Uke** is translated *Rising Block*. It is sometimes called Jōdan Age Uke, or Upper-Level Rising Block, to emphasize it goes up. Age Uke is used only in Nidan, where it is done 6 times, 3 each on the right and left. This block is useful for an overhead attack, for example a beer bottle coming straight down.

Be careful in pronouncing age. It's especially easy to confuse the pronunciation when the word is spelt like an English word. Don't pronounce it like how old you are. The word is two syllables, "ah gay". Sometimes writers will put an accent on the E to distinguish it from the English word: agé, as is sometimes done with saké, to distinguish it from sake, as in "For the sake of clarity". If your Japanese friends think you're always talking about the weather, you might be pronouncing Uke wrong. The E sounds like the English A, so "ah gay oo kay". That's "oo kay", not "oo key", which means 'rainy season'.

If you look up "block" in the dictionary, you won't find uke. If you look up "uke", you won't find block. It sounds strange at first, but the word uke actually means *receive*. In demonstrations and practice, especially in Aikidō and Jūdō, the uke is the receiver of the technique, i.e. the one thrown onto the floor. This would explain why virtually all martial artists agree it is better to give than to receive.

Training Notes for Age Uke

- As always: **Keep Low.**
- **The hands should** pass on the way up.
- The rising fist goes almost **straight up**, like you're punching the ceiling, and snaps at the last second, deflecting the blow, not meeting it.
- All movement should stop at the **same instant.**
- Tense at the moment of impact, then **relax.**

Mae Geri—Front Thrust Kick

Mae Geri is the *Front Kick*. An important observation: your legs are stronger than your arms and your legs are longer than your arms. This means you can reach someone with a kick from farther away, and the blow will be more damaging. Mae Geri is the only kick in the Taikyoku kata, and appears in Nidan and Yondan. Mae means *front*, and is written with the same kanji as the zen of Zenkutsu, Front Stance. Keri means kick, but becomes geri because of the consonant shift. Remember it's pronounced "Gary", not "Jerry".

The Chinese distinguish their styles with the saying "Kicks North, punches South", since the styles of northern China tend to kick, while the South, which had more contact with Okinawa, is noted for powerful punches. Korea, and thus Tae Kwon Do, was influenced by Northern styles, and TKD is noted for its kicks. The spirit of eclecticism that characterizes WKK is shown in kicks: The adoption of fluid kicking techniques from Tae Kwon Do are evident when Wadō Ki Kai kumite is observed. The most celebrated technique of this style, and one that it is best known for, is the front thrust kick. In our style, the kick is a thrust kick, not a snap kick. In Japanese, that's expressed as a Kekomi, not a Keage. You can practice the thrust kick by placing objects on a table and pushing them with the foot. To thrust, the hips must be powerfully involved, and the supporting foot should rotate as the heel follows the kick.

Proper kicking requires good balance. Some ideas to work on your balance: Put on your shoes and socks without sitting down; Stand on buses and commuter trains, such as BART trains. Practice your kick in a swimming pool; Try holding on to a wall at first to remove balance issues.

The kick has four distinct parts:

1. Lift the knee up high.
2. Exte-e-e-e-end the foot to strike with the ball of the foot.
3. Return the leg to the knee up position.
4. Put the leg back down (or kick again, to catch your opponent off guard).

Training Notes for Mae Geri

- All **four parts**.
- Keep the **toes up**; strike with the ball of the foot.
- Use the **Hips**.
- Work on your **balance**.

Gyaku Zuki—Reverse Punch

Gyaku Zuki is the *Reverse Punch*. It's called reverse because it is the reverse of Oi Zuki and because the sides of the arm and leg reverse. In a right Oi Zuki, the right hand and right foot will be forward at the moment of impact, camel-like. In the right Reverse Punch, on the other hand (no pun intended), the right hand and left foot will be forward. We will see it again in Yondan.

Gyaku means *inverted, reverse* or *opposite*, and can also mean *wicked*. You should strive to achieve this last definition in this technique: a Wicked Reverse Punch. Zuki is the same Zuki in Oi Zuki, and is a phonetic shift from Tsuki, so it is sometimes written Dzuki.

As with Oi Zuki, the fist should twist to face upward at the moment of contact. The twist should be delayed until just before contact to impart maximum torque.

Training Notes for Gyaku Zuki

- As always: **Keep Low.**
- **Don't lean forward** to reach the opponent. If you can't reach, you're too far away; move in, or kick instead of punch.
- **Delay the twist of the fist** until the last moment before contact.
- All movement should stop at the **same instant.**
- Tense at the moment of impact, then **relax.**

A Most Common Combo

Interestingly enough, the combination we learn in Nidan uses what are probably the two most useful individual attacks in Karate, Gyaku Zuki and Mae Geri, which together are probably the most useful combination. C.W. Nicol tells us that at the Shotokan in Tokyo, "the techniques that won more contests than any other were not the spectacular high kicks or difficult strikes, but rather the basic reverse punch and front kick."

> I tried then to develop these two techniques strongly, and concentrated on them to the neglect of others. The reverse punch, or 'gyaku-zuki', is usually delivered from a front stance, or 'zenkutsu-dachi.' It is a deep stance, with hips low, and with the leading leg bent so that the leading knee is over the toe of the leading foot. It was the first fighting stance taught at our school. If the left foot is forward, then the punch is delivered with the right fist. Delivered properly, it is an extremely fast and powerful blow, a killing blow, for in its focus, all the strength of the body is mustered.
>
> The front kick, or 'mae-geri,' is also usually delivered from the 'zenkutsu-dachi' stance. The kick is fast, too quick for the foot to be

caught. The opponent is struck by the ball of the foot, anywhere from the shin to the face. It is the first kick taught to the karateka.[48]

Training for Power

DEFINITION of Power, Relative to Karate:

1. (Force) x (Velocity)
2. (Strength) x (Speed)
3. The force and speed with which one is able to contract the muscle fibers.

General conditioning is important to the athlete in the early stages of training, in order to develop the necessary strength base needed to avoid injury. As the athlete develops, it is important that the conditioning program also develop. The exercise should build upon the strength base, and incorporate movements specific to the sport. This is known as sport specific training.

First, it is vital to identify abilities and characteristics required to excel in your sport. The martial artist must develop the following:

Balance
Kinesthetic Awareness
Control
Strength / Speed / Power

Once identified you can begin to design an effective program to enhance your performance. Compound exercises, particularly free weight exercises, will be most effective, as they most closely resemble life. For the advanced individual, machines can be limiting in their movement, and hinder the development of the desired sport specific characteristics.

Following are two programs that will help develop the characteristics inherent to an advanced martial artist.

INTERMEDIATE PROGRAM

Warmup	
Stationary Bike	15 min.
UBE	5 min.
Squat	2 x 10
Split Squat	2 x 6
Dumbbell Row	2 x 10
Bench Hurdles	3 x 20
Dumbbell Press	2 x 10
Dumbbell Lateral Raise	2 x 10
Dumbbell Bicep Curl	2 x 10
Dumbbell Tricep Extension (one arm / supine)	2 x 10
Abdominal Crunch	3 x 20

ADVANCED PROGRAM

Warmup	
Stairmaster (INT.)	10 min.
Lat Pulldown	10 min.
Squat / Pushpress	3 x 10
Lunge	3 x 10
Dumbbell Pullover	3 x 10
Overhead Throw	3 x 15
Incline Dumbbell Press	3 x 10
Power Drop	
Plyo Push-up	3 x 15
Bent Lateral Raise	3 x 10
Barbell Bicep Curl	3 x 10
Dumbbell Tricep Extension (overhead)	3 x 10
Abdominals	4 x 25

Variation on Nidan

The one source for Nidan, Funakoshi, in *Kyōhan*, shows a different Nidan than Wadō Ki Kai uses: "The foregoing description refers to Taikyoku Shodan. The following modify these instructions to produce Taikyoku Nidan...: The sequence of Taikyoku Nidan is identical to that of Shodan except that in Nidan, all punches are upper level instead of middle level attacks."[49] So this version of Nidan is much more like a kihon exercise, with nothing new, just some minor variations on the techniques already learned. WKK, on the other hand, includes new, useful techniques.

Kumite

Kumite or sparring is a way of practicing Karate techniques with a partner. Although our school does not emphasize sport Karate, sparring is an important aspect of our training in the development of technique, attitude, coordination, distance, and judgment.

If this were a more advanced book, we'd have a section in each chapter on sparring. But since White Belts don't spar, we skip it in most of the other chapters. Since beginners do not spar until they get past the basics, this book will not have a lot about kumite in it. However, it might be useful to let you hear a little from Musashi to get you thinking. Here's an excerpt from "The Ring of Fire", Patrick's translation:

Three Ways to Take the Lead

There are only three ways you can take the lead in a battle: 1. You can make a preemptive strike and attack the enemy; 2. You can wait and counterpunch when the enemy attack has faltered; or 3. You can simultaneously attack as the enemy attacks you.

These are the ways a battle can start. If you gain the upper hand, you might win quickly, so this is critical in military science. It's tricky to pull off, and can't be explained fully, but it's something you'll acquire with experience: the ability to grasp the situation, and know intuitively what the enemy will do.

1. Preemptive Strike

There are several ways you might accomplish a preemptive strike on the enemy:

- Lull the enemy with seeming inactivity, making it look like you're not planning anything, then attack suddenly and violently.
- Seemingly attack with all your force, but have a reserve ready.
- Attack with all your strength, with great speed in the attack.
- With calm determination, keep victory your constant goal.

In Japanese, this is called *ken no sen*.

2. Wait and Counterpunch

Make it appear you are weak and wait for the enemy to attack. When the attack starts, keep cool. When he's close, appear to collapse. When you've drawn him in, and he thinks you're retreating, hit him hard. Another approach is to wait until you sense a change in the attack's momentum, then answer the attack with all you've got. In Japanese, this is called *tai no sen*.

3. Simultaneous Attack

Here are a few examples of this technique. When the enemy attacks quickly, appear to be about to fall back, then feint an attack. While he's off guard, go for a decisive strike. Or meet a routine attack with a burst of force and drive home to victory. In Japanese, this is called *taitai no sen*. "Beat him to the punch".

There's a lot of intuition and judgment involved in deciding which lead to use, so it's not possible to write about them clearly. Try to get the general drift of the techniques from the book then you can acquire the rest through training. Each kind of response is appropriate in certain circumstances. You don't always have to initiate the attack, but if you do you'll put the enemy on the defensive. You need to work on this if you are going to be a successful fighter.

Dojo Lore

All dojo have rules, written or unwritten. As an example, these are the rules at Wadō Ki Kai.

Dojo Rules and Regulations

Rules and regulations have developed over the years to maximize learning and minimize injuries. The following is a partial list of some of the important rules to remember while training.

1. Be polite and respectful towards everybody at the Dōjō at all times
2. For safety consideration especially, obey your teacher's instructions at all times
3. Bow upon entering and leaving the Dōjō.
4. Bare feet only on the floor of the Dōjō (no street shoes). Do not go bare footed around any other area of the gym. Put your shoes or sandals on upon leaving the Dojo.
5. Practice *only* what you have been taught by a Black Belt instructor. Do not ask higher ranking classmates to show you parts of a kata or sparring techniques that the head instructor has not shown you first.
6. Class orderliness is important both for safety and learning purposes. Clowning around interferes with everyone's progress. Humor is at times warranted, but it is the instructor who should set the tone of each class.
7. No food or gum of any type is allowed on the floor. Please discard any of these items before entering the training area.
8. Wear a plain white, traditional Karate Gi while training. The only additional feature allowed on your Gi is the Wadō Ki Kai emblem.
9. Proper physical and oral hygiene including clipped toenails and fingernails are essential for mutual safety and respect. Plantar warts, athlete's foot, etc. are transmittable. So, if you have them, get rid of them! Wash your Gi and yourself regularly. And please, use deodorant.
10. Absolutely no sparring unless a Black Belt instructor is present.
11. Remove all jewelry before class begins. It is an unhappy occurrence for all when a cherished keepsake breaks. Also, these items can cause cuts and punctures to yourself or *to others* which at times can be serious.
12. Control your temper. Physical and mental self-control are integral components of martial arts practice.
13. Do not use more force than is necessary to help your training partners learn their moves and techniques. Good training is built on a positive attitude not a negative one.
14. Know your own limitations. Practice should be hard. But if you become genuinely fatigued, slow down. Use your judgment. If the pace of a class is too fast for your level of fitness or for any condition or injury you might have, slow down.
15. Foul or insulting language is not permitted.
16. Students should never use their skills except in self-defense.

17. If for *any* reason you need to leave the Dojo during class, tell a Black Belt instructor that you are leaving and why.

18. Report all injuries to the Sensei immediately regardless of how minor they may seem. Blood and body fluids should be treated as potentially infectious (HIV, hepatitis). Do not give aid to a person without taking adequate precautions, i.e., gloves. If you are injured and bleeding, leave the floor until the bleeding has completely stopped.

Nidan Controversies

Blocks As Attacks

Note the wings end with blocks, not punches. This seems odd, doesn't it? You seem to have left those opponents standing. Until you understand that "A block can be an attack". In fact Schmeisser, quoting Tony Annesi tells us "A block is a lock is a blow is a throw."[50] Nakayama, in *Dynamic Karate* elaborates: "As mentioned, a block can also serve as an attack. For example, a powerful block can deliver a shock strong enough to discourage further attack. There is another sense, however, in which blocking movements can serve as attacks. For instance, as the forearm blocks, the hand of the blocking arm can simultaneously strike the opponent's nose or chin. This characteristic of karate is absent from other martial arts."

In this technique specifically, Nakayama tells us "The upper block can be used as an attack in the following way. When the opponent attacks your head with a punch, lower your hips, lean slightly forward and step in under the attacking arm. At the same time apply the upper block in such a way that you simultaneously attack his armpit with your elbow and his chin with the bottom of his fist." And "Another possibility for the upper block as an attack occurs immediately after blocking. With the hand of your blocking arm, grasp the wrist of the opponent's attacking arm and pull downward, simultaneously applying the upper block with your other arm to his elbow joint."[51] And Burgar tells us that "Just about every block in traditional karate has a preparatory movement. These movements can be used as the actual block or entry into the opponent and what is traditionally regarded as the actual blocking movement is now used as a strike."[52]

Ikken Hissatsu Controversy

One of the principles of Karate is "Ikken Hissatsu" which literally means "One fist, certain death", and is usually translated something like "One punch decides the issue". Sensei Arce expresses this as "There should be only two hits in a real fight: You hit him, he hits the floor." Ikken Hissatsu is the nub of the "Ippon controversy", referring to the method employed in scoring Karate matches in which the first person to strike is awarded Ippon, or One Point, on the assumption that the opponent's counterpunch could never have landed, and further fighting is impossible, since the first strike would have been decisive and ended the contest. This is arguable, since we have the example of the Western-style boxing match where many blows are landed before the decisive knockout punch. Numerous jabs wear the opponent down before a final hook decides the match. In an Ippon contest, an opponent might land a blow that would not have disabled the other fighter, but will nonetheless win the match. In a real fight, a conditioned opponent might even invite a blow, tense to receive it harmlessly, then deliver a devastating counterpunch that truly is decisive. Choki Motobu, a giant of a man, would offer openings, inviting his opponent to take his best shot. If the opponent could reach him, he could reach them. His punch would not be as fast, nor as elegant, but anyone receiving it would gain deep and lasting insight into the concept of Ikken Hissatsu! So although a first attack can end a fight, it is certainly possible for a fight to continue beyond one blow, although the extended contests seen in the typical Kung Fu movie, each opponent absorbing numerous blows any one of which would kill a charging rhinoceros, go a bit too far.

Ikken Hissatsu is supported by two features of Okinawan Karate that we, thankfully, don't stress in WKK, *makiwara* and *tameshiwari*. The makiwara is a punching board that is pounded over and over, thousands of times, as the knuckles are bloodied then scarred, the bone itself actually calloused. In tameshiwari, the karateka breaks bricks, boards and tiles barehanded. Both of these support Ikken, since a blow that would shatter a pile of bricks will certainly kill someone if delivered to a vulnerable point.

During World War II, Taiheiyō Sensō—The Pacific War—the Japanese strategy was to seek the decisive battle, while the United States used an island-by-island strategy of attrition, bypassing strongpoints when possible. In this case at least, the Western style wear-them-down strategy was superior to the unsuccessful quest for the victory in decisive battle, the most horrific example of which was the Battle of Okinawa, which led to the death of tens of thousands of Japanese and Okinawans, but did not win the war for Japan.

Patrick for one is not interested in makiwara or tameshiwari, and we think it is wise in any event to expect that in a self-defense situation you should be prepared to hit your opponent more than once, and should certainly not drop your guard after a single blow, no matter how decisive you think it might have been.

Nidan Philosophy

Ki is the Key

An important concept in Karate is Ki. Ki means spirit, and encompasses all that word means in English, and more. Ki is the Ki in Wadō Ki Kai and also appears in two important words, Kime and Kiai. **Kime** is a Focus of Power, especially at the finish; an explosive attack to the target using the appropriate technique and maximum power in the shortest possible time. **Kiai** is a Manifestation of Ki—a simultaneous union of spirit and expression of physical strength. It is usually accompanied by a shout delivered for the purpose of focusing all of one's energy into a single movement and as an expression of the energy of the will. Even when audible Kiai are absent, one should try to preserve the feeling of Kiai at certain crucial points within Karate techniques.

Yin & Yang

Taikyoku is the First Principle of Chinese philosophy, and the Yin and the Yang spring from it. In fact, "Taikyoku" is also a name for the Yin Yang symbol, ☯. Yin/Yang is called Inyō in Japanese, as Yin became In, Yang Yō. It also forms the background of the Wadō Ki Kai logo and patch.

Yin and Yang are represented by the dark and light areas in the circle. Notice there is a little piece of light in the dark, and vice versa. This is because there is always a little bit of Yin in every Yang: there is light within the dark, strong within the weak, good within the evil, and vice versa. These Yin/Yang pairs are sometimes called opposites, but that is not accurate—they are actually complementary. One could not exist without the other. John Pereira said in his poem *Technique*: "The darkness of the sky makes the stars bright, complementing each other in the night." The stars are just as bright in the daytime as at night, only we can't see them without the contrast of the darkness of the sky.

Sensei Ferol Arce always emphasizes a punch is made more effective by the retreating hand, so both the so-called Yin and Yang hands are critical to the technique.

As a young Martial Artist then living in Oakland, California, said in his 1963 book: "The 'one-ness' of Yin/Yang is necessary in life. If a person riding a bike wishes to go somewhere, he cannot pump on both pedals at the same time or not pump on them at all. In order to move forward, he has to pump one pedal and release the other. So the movement of going forward requires this 'oneness' of pumping and releasing."[53] Incidentally, this particular Martial Artist later left Oakland to pursue a career in entertainment, of all things. Apparently, he even made a movie or two. His name was Bruce Lee.

A Good Ford

Another word from Musashi is in order here (Patrick's Interpretation):

> Often you'll have to cross a river, either literally or figuratively. The crossing can be rough and the crossing can be wide. Many times in your life, you'll be confronted with a situation that is a kind of crossing. You need to know the route, the capacity of the boat and the weather forecast. When you set out alone, taking advantage of good wind and currents, but be ready to row for a few miles if the wind goes out short of land.
>
> As you go through life, think of each challenge as a river crossing. Think of a battle as a river crossing. Consider your enemy's capabilities and your own readiness, and using what you've learned, cross the river at a good ford, like a master navigator crossing the sea. If you cross at a good ford, you can rest easy. Attack the enemy's weak points, using every advantage you can. Whether in individual combat or large-scale battles, the attitude of overcoming obstacles, crossing the river, is essential.

Nihongo

Japanese is built up from syllables, rather than letters. In English, we can combine a consonant with any vowel, but not so Japanese. There are fewer than 100 possible syllables in Modern Standard Japanese, as compared with thousands in English. In fact, a Japanese dictionary is arranged by syllables, so any Japanese grammar school student can rattle off all the possible syllables faster than a White Belt can do Taikyoku Yondan. Strange as it sounds to an English speaker, there are consonants in Japanese that cannot be combined with some vowels. For example, a Japanese can say "say". A Japanese can say "sah". A Japanese can say "sue". A Japanese can say "so". But a Japanese can NOT say "see"! Instead, it comes out "she". The sound of an English S followed by E or a short I becomes *Sh*, try as the Japanese may to make it sound like an S. As a smart-aleck schoolboy in Okinawa, Patrick found the Japanese accent hilarious and enticed Japanese to try to say "sit" as often as possible: "Please shit on the couch" or "Tokyo is a big shitty". When Japanese try to say "sit", well, "shit" happens. Two problems exist with T. "tah" is okay. "tay" is fine. "Toe" works. But "tea" becomes *chi*. And "two" becomes *tsu*. And "ha", "he", "hey" and "hoe" all come out fine. But "who" becomes *fu*.

Tiny tsu

A third, and, thankfully, final phonetic shift. Ikken is ichi, or *one*, combined with Ken. The ichi becomes Ik in the Hepburn System. In Ippon, ichi becomes Ip. Surprisingly, this is not inconsistent in Japanese since the double consonant stands for a semi-vowel that doesn't occur in English and the inconsistency is an artifact of the transliteration into English, not the Japanese language. The double consonant is actually written in Japanese with a small version of the syllable Tsu. Ts is one consonant that gives English speakers problems. It is the Tsu of tsunami, which most Americans pronounce as if it were *sunami*, simply dropping the T sound. The sound does occur in English, however. It occurs in spoken English, for example, when someone says "It's a deal!". It usually comes out "ih tsa deal". The sound of that tsa is what you're after.

In any event, the Japanese use a small tsu in writing to stand for another sound English speakers find problematical, the semi-vowel Dr. Hepburn chose to represent by doubling the consonant that follows it. It actually is a pause, closer to a stutter than anything else. Most people can't stutter on demand, but you can get pretty close to the correct sound if you put the consonant on both syllables. Ikken should distinctly sound like "Seek Ken", never like "See Ken". We spell Potsai, the name of the kata, the way we do instead of Passai, as many ryu do, since an English speaker tends to say "Pass eye" instead of the correct "Pot Tsai".

Counting

Ippon Ikken

Hon, used to count long slender objects such as pencils and sticks, is also used for arms, and points in a match: one point, ippon; two, nihon; three sambon. It really demonstrates the strangeness of phonetic shifts. You'll note the H in Hon sometimes becomes P, sometimes becomes B, and sometimes remains H. For now, you'd probably better just memorize them. You'll find it very useful, because it's also used to count bottles of beer. "Biiru nihon!": "Two beers".

#	Points
1	Ippon
2	Nihon
3	Sambon
4	Shihon
5	Gohon
6	Roppon
7	Shichihon or Nanahon
8	Happon or Hachihon
9	Kyūhon
10	Jippon

Nidan Kanji

Uke Kanji

As we mentioned, this word literally means not block, but receive. That's supposed to be a hand, Te, on top, but it looks mangled. The inventor of this kanji apparently drank too much sake while trying to invent the computer then got the hand caught in a loom. Think of it this way: The top piece can be a knuckle, hitting a shield. Bottom signifies a nice front stance, knee over the foot, back leg locked. The knuckle is stopped by the shield of front stance, in keeping with the sage advice offered by the great sage of fighting: Don't get hit.

4.

WIND: Taikyoku Sandan

"Military Science involves knowledge of the methods of other schools."
"Unless you know the ways of other schools, you certainly cannot understand the way of my individual school."[54]
—Miyamoto Musashi, describing Kaze no Rin, the Ring of Wind.

Seeking

The theme of this chapter is learning from others, and thus tolerance. We practice a style of Karate called Wadō Ki Kai. The poetic translation is "To Learn from All Things". This system of Karate is a combination of traditional and contemporary styles of training made by our late teacher, Master John Pereira, 8th Dan. Wadō Ki Kai is primarily an Okinawan-Japanese system, but it incorporates other aspects of different styles of martial arts. Traditional katas from Shorinji-Ryu, Shotokan, Gojukai, and Wado-Ryu, are included. In addition, Okinawan weaponry, Chinese Kung-Fu weapons, and Korean kicking techniques from Tae Kwon Do are included. Sensei Pereira passed away in 1993. It is our hope to carry on the legacy he left us, and share it with others. Since our goal is To Learn from All Things, in this chapter we will consider other styles.

Just a thought to help you open your mind to other ideas and cultures: If this book is your first exposure to Japanese, you're probably thinking Japanese is crazy. Listen to Richard Lederer, who in *Crazy English* tells us that all languages, including English, are a little crazy. "Still, you have to marvel at the unique lunacy of the English language, in which your house can simultaneously burn up and burn down, in which you fill in a form by filling out a form, in which you add up a column of figures by adding them down, in which your alarm clock goes off by going on, in which you inoculate for measles by being inoculated against measles, and in which you first chop a tree down—and then you chop it up." "That's because language is invented, not discovered, by boys and girls and men and women, not computers. As such, language reflects the creativity and fearful asymmetry of the human race, which, of course, isn't really a race at all."[55]

Taikyoku Sandan Choreography

#	Side	Waza	Technique	Tachi	Notes
1	Left	Chūdan Ude Uke	Middle Forearm Block	Kōkutsu	90° Left Turn
2	Right	Gamen Shutō Uchi	Circular Knife-Edge Strike	Zenkutsu	
3	Right	Chūdan Ude Uke	Middle Forearm Block	Kōkutsu	180° Right Turn
4	Left	Gamen Shutō Uchi	Circular Knife-Edge Strike	Zenkutsu	
5	Left	Gedan Barai	Down Block	Zenkutsu	90° Left Turn
6a	Right	Yoko Chūdan Zuki	Side Middle Punch	Kiba	
6b	Right	Gedan Uraken Uchi	Down Block-Knuckle Strike	Kiba	Shutō Chest
7a	Left	Yoko Chūdan Zuki	Side Middle Punch	Kiba	
7b	Left	Gedan Uraken Uchi	Down Block-Knuckle Strike	Kiba	Shutō Chest
8a	Right	Yoko Chūdan Zuki	Side Middle Punch	Kiba	
8b	Right	Gedan Uraken Uchi	Down Block-Knuckle Strike	Kiba	**Kiai!** Shutō Chest
09	Left	Chūdan Ude Uke	Middle Forearm Block	Kōkutsu	270° Left Turn
10	Right	Gamen Shutō Uchi	Circular Knife-Edge Strike	Zenkutsu	
11	Right	Chūdan Ude Uke	Middle Forearm Block	Kōkutsu	180° Right Turn
12	Left	Gamen Shutō Uchi	Circular Knife-Edge Strike	Zenkutsu	
13	Left	Gedan Barai	Down Block	Zenkutsu	90° Left Turn
14a	Right	Yoko Chūdan Zuki	Side Middle Punch	Kiba	Heading Home
14b	Right	Gedan Uraken Uchi	Down Block-Knuckle Strike	Kiba	Shutō Chest
15a	Left	Yoko Chūdan Zuki	Side Middle Punch	Kiba	
15b	Left	Gedan Uraken Uchi	Down Block-Knuckle Strike	Kiba	Shutō Chest
16a	Right	Yoko Chūdan Zuki	Side Middle Punch	Kiba	
16b	Right	Gedan Uraken Uchi	Down Block-Knuckle Strike	Kiba	**Kiai!** Shutō Chest
17	Right	Chūdan Ude Uke	Middle Forearm Block	Kōkutsu	270° Left Turn
18	Left	Gamen Shutō Uchi	Circular Knife-Edge Strike	Zenkutsu	
19	Left	Chūdan Ude Uke	Middle Forearm Block	Kōkutsu	180° Right Turn
20	Right	Gamen Shutō Uchi	Circular Knife-Edge Strike	Zenkutsu	

See the kata performed at www.wadokikai.com.

Taikyoku Sandan Techniques

Chudan Ude Uke	中段腕受け	Middle forearm Block
Gamen Shuto Uchi	画面手刀打ち	Circular Knife-edge Strike
Gedan Barai	下段払い	Down Block
Gedan Uraken Uchi	下段裏拳打ち	Downward Block-Knuckle Strike
Kiba Dachi	騎馬立ち	Horse stance
Kokutsu Dachi	後屈立ち	Back Stance
Yoko Chudan Zuki	横中段突き	Side Middle Punch
Zenkutsu Dachi	前屈立ち	Front Stance

Shinkokata Number 3

From Gedan Barai (Down Block) Gamen Shutō Uchi (Circular Knife-Edge Strike) in Zenkutsu Dachi (Front Stance).

Command	Technique	Note
Yōi.	Ready Stance	
Hajime!	Left Gedan Barai	
(Ichi)	Right Gamen Shutō Uchi	
(Ni)	Left Gamen Shutō Uchi	
(San)	Right Gamen Shutō Uchi	
(Shi)	Left Gamen Shutō Uchi	
(Go)	Right Gamen Shutō Uchi	Kiai!
Kaesu!	Left Gedan Barai	180° Turn to the Left Counterclockwise
(Ichi)	Right Gamen Shutō Uchi	
(Ni)	Left Gamen Shutō Uchi	
(San)	Right Gamen Shutō Uchi	
(Shi)	Left Gamen Shutō Uchi	
(Go)	Right Gamen Shutō Uchi	Kiai!
Yame.	Ready Stance	

Dojo Lore

WKK Influences

Naha-te, Goju, Shuri-te, and Shoto are all manifest in the Wadō Ki Kai system. Traditional katas from Shorinji-Ryu, Shotokan, Gojukai, and Wado-Ryu are included.

In the spirit of understanding, the table shows other ways to name the kata. The column headed Olde Okinawa shows some of the spelling variations. For example, Kusanku and Kanku are variations on the same name, as in fact are Kosokun, Kōshōkun, Kushanku, Kankū, Koushoukun and Kwankū (feel free to make up your own way of spelling it). In the column headed "Japanese" you'll see the Modern Standard Japanese (MSJ) rendering, or the name used by the JKA (Shotokan).

As with most things, we at Wadō Ki Kai are true to the Okinawan roots of the art. For example, we use the traditional name Pingan instead of Heian, Nahanchi instead of Tekki, Potsai instead of Bassai, Chinto instead of Gankanku, Kusanku instead of Kanku, and Seisan instead of Hangetsu. The only exception is Empi, for which we do not use the original Wanshu. Note the chart gives our current research on the names and kanji. Much of this is lost in history and controversy, so other assignments are possible. Please forgive us if we did not use your favorite rendering, but we're always open to new information if you'd care to provide it to us.

Note the switching of Pingan Shodan and Nidan. What was originally Shodan is now Nidan in most styles, and Nidan is Shodan.

I trust that the Repetition will Forge the Spirit: We do it Over and Over to get Better and Better.

The Wadō Ki Kai Kata

#	Belt	WKK	Olde Okinawan	Kanji	Japanese	Kanji	Meaning
1	White	Taikyoko Shodan	Same	太極初段	Same	太極初段	Focus Mind, Body and Spirit (Beginning Level)
2	White	Taikyoko Nidan	Same	太極二段	Same	太極二段	Focus Mind, Body and Spirit (Level 2)
3	White	Taikyoko Sandan	Same	太極三段	Same	太極三段	Focus Mind, Body and Spirit (Level 3)
4	White	Taikyoko Yo(n)dan	Same	太極四段	Same	太極四段	Focus Mind, Body and Spirit (Level 4)
5	Yellow	Pingan Shodan	Pin(')an Nidan	平安二段	Heian Shodan	平安初段	Peaceful Mind (Beginning Level)
6	Yellow	Pingan Nidan	Pin(')an Shodan	平安初段	Heian Nidan	平安二段	Peaceful Mind (Level 2)
7	Yellow	Pingan Sandan	Pin(')an Sandan	平安三段	Heian Sandan	平安三段	Peaceful Mind (Level 3)
8	Orange	Pingan Yo(n)dan	Pin(')an Yo(n)dan	平安四段	Heian Yo(n)dan	平安四段	Peaceful Mind (Level 4)
9	Orange	Pingan Godan	Pin(')an Godan	平安五段	Heian Godan	平安五段	Peaceful Mind (Level 5)
10	Orange	Nahanchi Shodan	Naif(u)anchi(n) Shodan	内蟠?地	Tekki Shodan	鉄騎初段	O: Holding Ground? J: Iron Horse (Begin Level)
11	Green	Jion	Same	慈恩	Same	慈恩	Temple Sound; Name of a temple
12	Green	Saifa	Saifa(a)	砕破	Saiha	砕破	Break and Tear; Final Breaking Point?
13	Blue	Potsai Dai	Passai Dai	抜塞大	Bassai Dai	抜塞大	Breach Fortress (Major)
14	Blue	Chinto	Chintō	鎮闘?	Gankaku	岩鶴	O: Name of a sailor? J: Crane on a Rock
15	Purple	Unsa	Uns(h)u	雲手	Unsu	雲手	Hand in Cloud
16	Purple	Empi	Wans(h)u	汪輯	Empi	燕飛	O: Name of an envoy J: Flying Swallow (the bird)
17	Brown 3rd Kyu	Seisan	Seis(h)an	十三手	Hangetsu	半月	O: 13 Hands J: Half Moon
18	Brown 3rd Kyu	Sushi No Sho [Bo]	S(h)(i)ushi no Kon				
19	Brown 3rd Kyu	Gay Pa [Sai]					
20	Brown 2nd Kyu	Kusanku Sho	Kōs(h)ōkun Shō	公相君小	Kankū Shō	観空小	O: Name of an official J: Viewing the Sky (Minor)
21	Brown 2nd Kyu	Soea [Sai]					
22	Brown 1st Kyu	Sakagawa Bo	Sakagawa Bō	佐久川棒	Sakagawa Bō	佐久川棒	Name of a famous karateka
23	Brown 1st Kyu	Giokerin [Sai]					

Sandan Technique

Sandan is the only Taikyoku kata that contains all three of the basic stances learned in the Taikyoku kata: Zenkutsu Dachi; Kōkutsu Dachi; and Kiba Dachi. It teaches stance differentiation. Unfortunately, many White Belts choose to invent a new stance. They seem to do a Zenko or Kozen Kutsu, half way between Zen- and Ko- kutsu.

Grant Butterfield trains his students to automatically think "It's different" every time they hear "Taikyoku Sandan" announced, because unlike the other three Taikyoku kata, Sandan starts in Kokutsu Dachi not Zenkutsu, and does not start with Gedan Barai.

Kōkutsu Dachi—Back stance

Kōkutsu Dachi is the *Back Stance*, literally the Back Bent Stance. The technique is used only in Taikyoku Sandan, and is usually thought of as a defensive position. Shift back into this position as you are attacked to evade the strike.

If you have a good Kokutsu, you can shift into Zenkutsu and back without relocating the feet. The back foot will rotate on the heel but stay in the same spot. The front foot points straight ahead, directly at the opponent, the back foot at 90 degrees. The body is at a 45-degree angle with the eyes focused on the opponent.

Training Notes for Kokutsu

- Keep Low.
- Don't lean forward.
- 60/40.

Chūdan Ude Uke—Middle Forearm Block

Ude Uke is the *Forearm Block*. This technique is a little tricky at first, because the movement comes from low to high, the opposite of the Gedan Barai that usually appears at that step of the kata. Think of this as a sweeping movement, sweeping the attack to the midsection or chin. As with Gedan Barai, though, don't sweep past the body. A good visualization is to imagine pulling a sword from a scabbard.

Training Notes for Ude Uke

- Settle in.
- Don't lean forward.

- You're in Kokutsu.
- Pull your sword out.
- Relax then Tense. Like a dog, growl before you bite!

Shutō—Sword Hand

Shutō literally means Hand Sword and is translated *Sword Hand*. The shu is an alternate pronunciation for our old friend Te.

The tō means *sword*. This character can also be read *ken*. We've seen that fist is also "ken". The pun has been called the lowest form of humor. Children's Valentine cards make jokes like "Bee my honey", exploiting the puns available from the honeybee. The Japanese, however, think there is significance in words that sound alike, so some karateka take advantage of the homophone to adapt samurai aphorisms about the sword to the fist.

Training Notes for Shuto

- Keep your **thumb in**.
- Keep your **fingers tight**.
- You're hitting your opponent's **neck**.

Gamen Shutō Uchi—Circular Knife-Edge Strike

Gamen Shutō Uchi is the *Circular Knife-Edge Strike*. The technique comes from the ear.

Don't lean forward to reach the opponent. If you can't reach, you're too far away; move in, or kick instead of punch. Make a full circle: The hand starts next to the ear, palm forward.

Training Notes for Shuto Uchi

- As always: **Keep Low**.
- **Don't lean forward** to reach the opponent.
- Make a **full circle**.

Kiba Dachi—Horse Stance

Kiba Dachi is literally "Horse-Riding Stance", so it's called Straddle-Leg Stance, or more commonly, *Horse Stance*. The stance is used in Taikyoku sandan and yondan, and also appears in the Naihanchi kata, so it is sometimes called the Naihanchi stance.

If you, like many beginners, are having trouble with this stance, take heart from the fact Funakoshi himself noted how hard it is to master: "The *kibadachi* ("horse-riding stance"), for instance, looks extremely easy but the fact is that no one could possibly master it even if he practiced every day for an entire year until his feet became as heavy as lead."[56]

This stance is literally strong enough to withstand a raging typhoon: "Now the young man on the roof assumed a low posture, holding the straw mat aloft against the raging wind. The stance he took was most impressive, for he stood as if astride a horse. Indeed, anyone who knew karate could readily have seen that the youth was taking the horse-riding stance, the most stable of all karate stances, and that he was making use of the howling typhoon to refine his technique and to further strengthen both body and mind. The wind struck the mat and the youth with full force, but he stood his ground and did not flinch."[57] This incident demonstrates the stability of Kiba Dachi, but as one who has experienced several typhoons, on Okinawa, and at sea, let me offer you a friendly piece of advice: Don't try this at home!

Training Notes for Kiba

- As with Zenkutsu Dachi, remember to **Keep Low**. Pretend like you're sitting on a stool.
- Don't lean forward: **shoulders back.**
- Keep the **feet parallel** to each other, as if they were on a railroad track, or more appropriately, in the stirrups of a horse.

Yoko Chūdan Zuki—Side Middle Punch

Yoko Zuki is the *Side Punch*. It is actually the same movement as Oi Zuki, just aimed to the side. The technique ends in Kiba Dachi. As with Oi and Gyaku Zuki, the fist should start at the belt and not twist downward until just before contact. As you step, the foot should also twist at the last moment to impart torque to the punch. It is as if you were going to go into the Ladies' Horse Stance, but changed your mind at the last moment. To work up to this move, you can practice actually stopping in Ladies' Horse Stance, then shifting. Then start shifting just before your foot lands.

Training Notes for Yoko Zuki

- As always: **Keep Low.**
- **Twist the foot** just before it lands.

- All movement should stop at the **same instant**.
- **Delay the twist of the fist** until the last moment before contact.

Gedan Uraken Uchi—Downward Block-Knuckle Strike

Gedan Uraken Uchi is the *Downward Block-Knuckle Strike.* Uraken, or Ura Ken, is the Back Fist. Ura means "the back or other side" and ken is the familiar fist. Uchi means strike or chop, and unlike a Tsuki, does not thrust, and does not have the elbow behind the blow.

In the preparation for the move, both hands should make a full, smooth circle. The blow should start high, with the arms and shoulders up. The Uraken's bunkai is to break the opponent's nose.

Training Notes for Uraken Uchi

- Similar to the regular punch, end with a snap, and **corkscrew at the last second**.
- The retreating hand is pulled down to the breastplate of the **chest in Shuto**.
- Big circle.
- Drop it on 'em
- Like a **dagger**, then twist the fist.
- **Keep Low.** Don't lean forward.

Variations on Sandan

The two books we used that were in English that include Sandan disagree with each other and with WKK. Tadashi Nakamura, however, does include Sandan in the Japanese version of *Karate: Technique & Spirit*, which the English version does not. His Sandan is the same as Mas Oyama's in *Karate School.*[58]

Funakoshi in *Kyōhan* looks at this kata in detail but it's different from WKK,[59] and Oyama. "In Taikyoku Sandan, the down blocks along Lines 1 and 3 of Taikyoku Shodan are replaced with middle level arm blocks (ude uke) executed in back (kōkutsu) stance, and the threefold sets of middle level front attacks along Line 2 become sets of upper level attacks, the remaining movements being identical to Taikyoku Shodan."[60] Note the first move, Ude Uke in Kōkutsu, is the same as WKK.

Kumite

Know Your Enemy

Even if you can't learn from your enemy, you'll need to understand him in order to defeat him. Patton read Rommel's book before defeating him. A quote from Musashi:

> In combat, whether between individuals or armies, you must strive to know your enemy. How's his morale? What are his intentions? What is the lay of the land? Determine the enemy's strength and disposition. Get good intelligence.
>
> Even in hand-to-hand combat, psych out your opponent, determine what his modus operandi is, and figure out his strengths and weaknesses. Try to surprise him by messing up his timing and catching him off guard. It takes time to develop this kind of intuition, an ability to read your opponent's mind, but you'll get it if you work at it.

Sandan Controversy

Strategy & Honesty

Funakoshi's birth date is somewhat uncertain. He says in his autobiography that he was born in 1868 despite the fact official records give 1870. He was too old to qualify for a school he wished to attend, and so "I had no alternative but to tamper with the official records".[61] He does not explain how this tampering was consistent with his precept "Karate fosters righteousness".

In his most famous encounter, Musashi fought and killed Sasaki Kojiro, inventor of his own style, Gan-Ryu, on Funa Jima (Jima means Island). This small island was later renamed Gan-Ryu Jima after Kojiro's school. Musashi used an oar, whittled into a Bokken on the trip to the island, instead of a sword. As Hidy Ochiai tells us "it was much remarked that Musashi deliberately came late for the encounter; Kojiro had to wait more than two hours for his opponent to arrive. Is this why people later felt more sympathy for Kojiro, and renamed the island in his memory? Musashi's detractors use this story to illustrate that there's an aspect of Musashi's strategy which is underhanded and unfair."[62] Ochiai defends Musashi, arguing that from his point of view: "Losing in combat normally meant death, so one must win at all costs. The combat starts the moment the agreement to meet with swords is made, not at the site of the combat." Yes, but the entire point of Bushidō is that there are higher things than one's own life. Surely Seppuku (hara-kiri) is the opposite of the viewpoint defended by Ochiai; many samurai chose to take their own lives in the name of honor. The title of this Chapter, Kaze, also appears in Kamikaze, the extreme, and even foolish, example of sacrificing one's own life to a higher cause.

Sandan Philosophy

The Way

To the samurai, being a warrior was a Way of life, or *Tao*. The word Tao, pronounced halfway between "Dah-Oh" and "Dow", means *path* or *way*, and came into Japanese as *dō*. You've encountered this word many times in this book, perhaps without realizing it. The "-dō" on the end of the Budō—martial arts— 道 including Jūdō, Kendō, and Aikidō are the very same *dō*. Some Karateka like to add Dō to Karate to get Karate-Dō, thus emphasizing that Karate is a Path to learning about oneself and the world, well beyond mere technique. It is the second character in Wadō Ki Kai. It also appears at the end of Bushido, the Way of the Warrior. It also appears in *dōjō*, which is a place where a *way* is taught. The *jō* simply means place, so a martial arts sensei (teacher) will teach at a dojo. It is also the *tō* at the end of Shintō. The character can also be pronounced michi, and is the michi in the kotowaza with which we opened this book, "Sen Ri no Michi mo Ippo kara"—"Even a journey of a Thousand Miles starts from One Step". The Japanese seem to be able to elevate anything to a way, there even being Sadō, the Way of Tea, as delightfully explained in Kakuzo Okakura's 1906 *The Book of Tea*.[63] A Way can be a way of life.

No discussion of the Way would be complete without a quote of the first verse of the *Tao Te Ching*, written by Lao Tzu:[64]

> The tao that can be told
> is not the eternal Tao.
> The name that can be named
> is not the eternal Name.

Many Ways to the Mountaintop

The Japanese are noted for their eclecticism and openness to ideas, and Japanese religion is no exception. Originally, Japan followed its native religion, Shintō, the Way of the Gods, while India followed Hinduism, and China followed a native religion based on ancestor worship. Then the three great founders of Asian religion appeared in the sixth century b.c.e.; dates are hazy, but it appears there was an overlap of about two decades (550-531 b.c.e.) in the lives of Lao Tzu (604-531), Confucius (551-479) and Siddhartha Gautama (550-480). For reference, Pythagoras was doing the square-of-the-hypotenuse, and Jeremiah and Ezekiel were active in Israel at this same time. In China, Lao Tzu—also spelt Laotzu, Lao Tse or Laotse—founded a religion later called Taoism, and Confucius established the ethic that takes his name. In India, Gautama, later called Buddha, established a sect of Hinduism that later became Buddhism. Buddhism eventually moved to China, where it mingled with Taoism, Confucianism, and the native religion. In this form it traveled to Japan where a syncretism with Shinto produced Japan's eclectic religious tradition. And after Japan's opening to the West, Japan assimilated many ideas from Western science and philosophy. So Japanese religious philosophy draws on Hinduism, Buddhism, Confucianism, Taoism, Shinto, and the tradition of ancestor worship, with some Western rationalism for flavor.

The early Christian missionaries were pleased when they easily won converts among the Japanese, who then earnestly requested crucifixes to take home to keep in the place of highest honor. But they were shocked to discover the place of highest honor was right next to the statue of Buddha. The Japanese saw no conflict between the two religions and so had no problem being both Christian and Buddhist. If you ask a Japanese "Are you Shinto, Buddhist, Taoist or Confucian", the answer will probably be "Yes".[65] According to the cliché, Japanese are born into Shintō, live their lives as Confucians, and die Buddhists. Babies are taken to the Shinto shrine soon after birth for a ceremony similar to Christening; the Japanese salaryman is the epitome of Confucian duty; and funerals are usually held at Buddhist temples.

When asked to compare various methods of attaining enlightenment, the Buddha is said to have remarked: "There are many ways to the Mountaintop." Some are harder, and some are easier; some are surer, some slipperier. But many ways are valid. This world would be a better place if we could all truly live this philosophy. It certainly is true of Karate: try to learn from other styles, as Johnny Pereira, the founder of Wadō Ki Kai encouraged. If life is a climb to the summit, you and I might take a different route, but we can both reach the top, and enjoy the view together when we both get there.

Bushidō

The most direct source of Samurai ethics is Bushidō, the Way of the Samurai. Japanese is written with ideograms that convey ideas that remain constant even as the pronunciation may change. The 'shi' in bu*shi*do is written with a character that means 'gentleman' or 'samurai'—bu, somewhat redundantly means military, and dō, means "Way". Japan had honored a warrior class in pre-Buddhist times.

Bushidō drew on all the Japanese tradition, but had two primary sources of especial interest when trying to understand the Samurai: Confucianism and Zen Buddhism. "As to strictly ethical doctrines, the teachings of Confucius were the most prolific source of Bushido."[66] Confucianism is often described as an ethic, not a religion. There was a raging controversy over several centuries within the Catholic Church (~1582-1742) on this very issue. The Jesuits, Franciscans and Dominicans were all attempting to gain converts in China. The Jesuits, believing in "the power to do good", tried to convert Chinese leaders, reasoning the populace would follow. The Franciscans and Dominicans were bottom up, preaching among the commoners. And so developed the Civil Rites (sic) Controversy. The Jesuits argued that Mandarins could convert to Catholicism and still retain their positions of influence, which required them to engage in rites and rituals of government, based on Confucian *ethics*, even as a Westerner might bow to his King, or take part in a parade on a national holiday. The other Orders insisted those were *religious* rites, and must be disavowed by Catholics, thus effectively removing Jesuit converts from power. In 1742, the Pope came down against the Jesuits, arguing Confucianism was religious, but it's an open question again today, as the modern world catches up with the Japanese concept of different, yet correct, ways.

The second major influence on Bushido was a particular version of Buddhism, strongly influenced by Taoism, the sect called Zen. This sect was very popular among the ruling warrior class, but the association of Zen with warriors is perhaps misleading. As Thomas Cleary observes, Zen is not necessarily martial: "In the relationship between Zen and the samurai, therefore, the teacher should not be assessed by the level of the student. If martial arts were really considered the highest form of study in Japan, as has been suggested by some apologists, Zen masters would have been students of the warriors, and not the other way around."[67]

Zen's stoicism suited the warrior, who might face death in battle, as well as the Samurai bureaucrat, who was more likely to die from boredom, as is the modern-day Samurai, the salaryman. "Salaryman" is what the Japanese call corporate employees. Note the use of 'man' in this context is gender neutral, and not sexist. The Japanese that use the term *salaryman* are rarely aware of the meaning of the two English words, salary and man, that compose it, just as Americans who use Japanese compounds like "kamikaze" and "hara-kiri" don't know *kami* means 'god', *kaze* means 'wind', *hara* means 'gut', and, *kiri* means 'cut'. In fact, Japanese syntax is devoid of gender distinctions, using gender-neutral honorifics based on relative social position instead. Note Japanese writers do not put spaces between words, so 'salaryman' may also be rendered 'salary man'. In the Hepburn transliteration, it is rendered 'sarariman'.

Nihongo

Long Vowels

Unfortunately, there is no good method for transliterating Japanese words into English. The greatest difficulty is representing the long vowels. Some vowels are marked as long, or are repeated, to denote a long vowel. Unlike in English, the long vowel is pronounced exactly the same as the short vowel, only the duration changes. The long vowel in Japanese actually sounds exactly the same as the short vowel, but it is held longer, to wit, for another syllable. So *do* (times) is one syllable, but dō (way) is two: dough-o-oh. Just hold the sound longer. And for ā (with a macron) or aa, instead of "Ah", like you might say upon enlightenment, say "Ahhh", like you'd say while the doctor is examining your throat. As with many things in Martial Arts, this is hard at first, but you'll get it with a little practice.

"Did you bring your hate with you today?"

That sentence doesn't make a lot of sense does it? Hate isn't something one decides to bring or leave behind. But what if the person explained: "Oops, I mixed my short and long vowels again! I meant hat, not hate: Did you bring your hat with you today?" This is not the kind of error we unconsciously correct for, because native English speakers never make an error of that type. We do not confound long and short vowels. The long vowels are formed differently in Japanese and English, but they are similar in that confusing them is not an error a native speaker makes, and so will not adjust for. So the long and the short of vowels is that if you make an error, the Japanese will be baffled—or worse.

Since we don't change the duration of our vowels in English, there is no good way to handle long vowels in text. It is designated in various methods with a macron (ō) or a circumflex (ô), or as oh. Too frequently books ignore the distinction and show them both the same—many typesets lose them, and publishers find them annoying and drop them. So if you are trying to avoid the assistant (komon)/anus (kōmon) problem you don't know how to pronounce a word. In this book we have chosen to represent lomng vowles with macrons, which is the most common way: kō, but since the macron is often used in English to denote the English long vowel sound, people think that's what they designate. The Takahashi dictionary uses the circumflex or hat: dôjô, which at least won't be mistaken for the English pronunciation mark. Some people use an h to denote a long vowel: Wadō Ryu founder Ohtsuka (Ōtsuka) Hironori; Chinteh for Chintei kata. Last but not least, people familiar with Japanese writing prefer to transliterate the characters one by one from hiragana. This will sometimes double the vowel, long A, I and log U are sometimes written aa, ii and uu. Long e is usually given as ei, but occasionally ee. In the case of O it will usually become ou. This presents problems, since dojo becomes doujou, and people try to pronounce it Dow Jow. When using this method, the long o is usually shown as ou, but in a few words it is written oo in Japanese. For some reason, the word big (ooki) is written with a double o, not ou. This is the Oo of Ōsaka, which would be written Oosaka. Note these are all questions of representation in English; the Japanese word is pronounced exactly the same whichever method is used.

The **Yoko** of Yoko Zuki means side, and is the Yoko of Yokohama. For approximately 250 years, Japan was *Sakoku*, a closed country. Foreigners were forbidden to enter the country. In 1853, Commodore Matthew C. Perry, U.S. Navy, arrived with his Black Ships. Since the might of the US Navy was impressive to the Japanese who'd fallen technologically far behind during their period of isolation, they were forced to sign the Treaty of Kanagawa allowing Western intrusion into the country. When Westerners first began moving to Japan in the 1850s, sunsequent treaties allowed them to stay in the port city of Kanagawa. The Japanese, however, did not particularly want the Westerners around. You probably wouldn't either. The Japanese have always had reverence for the bath, while a European of that time might not take a single bath during an entire lifetime! And the Japanese didn't, and still don't, understand the handkerchief. "Those Westerners are strange: They save their boogers!" Kleenex is one American company that sells very successfully to Japanese, because they like to throw away the discharge after blowing their noses, and are baffled that anyone would carry a snotty rag around in their pocket. In any event, the Japanese of Kanagawa decided to relegate the Stinking Barbarians to the other 'side of the harbor', or 'yoko hama'. The Yokohamans had the last laugh, however, since Yokohama grew to be much more important than Kanagawa, which has since been absorbed into Yokohama and does not exist as a separate city anymore.

Thrust or Strike

Patrick's father was in the Air Force. I was lucky to live in many places as I grew up. I spent about half my growing years in the Far East. One of the most beneficial results of this was exposure to another culture, and thus ways of looking at the world. I have always been willing to challenge accepted beliefs, and I think observing that another culture could successfully solve many problems in a completely different way than Westerners do led to a better thought process, and certainly more tolerance, than I might have developed otherwise."

As an example of how two cultures can look at the same thing differently, consider the example of eating (taberu) and drinking (nomu). As Takao Suzuki points out in *Words in Context*,[68] the two concepts almost, but not quite, match up between English and Japanese. In English, the concept distinguishing the two words is whether the substance consumed is solid or liquid. In Japanese, however, the distinction is whether or not the substance is chewed. The vast majority of the time, the two match, since we usually chew solids (eat = taberu) and do not chew liquids (drink = nomu). But in some instances they do not match up. Nomu, "drink", more precisely means "to take into the body without chewing", which is why a Japanese will "drink" a cigarette. It is also possible to drink rice: for example, if someone has a fishbone caught in his throat, he might drink some rice, that is gulp some rice without chewing it to dislodge the bone. Another example is aoi, a word that is both the color of the sky, what in English is called "blue", and the color of grass, or "green". The colors of the rainbow have been arbitrarily divided differently in the two languages, with blue, blue-green, and green all becoming aoi. An example from family relationships is brother. There is no word for brother in Japanese. There is a word that means older brother (ani), and a word that means younger brother (otōto). Because the relationship to an older brother is quite different from that to a younger brother, the Japanese culture considers them so dissimilar as to require a different word. In America, there isn't as much difference between the two kinds of brother, and there is only one word for the two.

This brings us to a distinction between two words, tsuki and uchi, in Japanese that is not the same in the English counterparts. In English, blows with the hand are divided based on the disposition of the hand: punch with a fist. An open hand will be a chop, slap or poke, depending on what part of the hand is striking. In Japanese the emphasis is on whether the elbow is behind the blow (tsuki, thrusting) or bent and snapping (uchi). Thus a blow with the back of the fist is a back punch in English, but an uchi, not a tsuki in Japanese, and a finger thrust, which in English would be a poke, not a punch, is a tsuki. Basically, if you drive the hand forward from the traditional Karate position at the side, you have a tsuki, no matter what you do with your hand and fingers.

Sandan Kanji

We'll use Kiba to introduce radicals. No, not political activists. Look at the second character in Kiba, it's a horse. See its legs, and tail, and mane? Try some sake. Look at the left half of the first character. It's also a horse, or at least it's the same character. In Japanese you need two dictionaries because you can't look up a word by its pronunciation because you don't know how to pronounce a kanji if you aren't familiar with it, so you look it up by its radical. Kanji with the same radical will be in a character dictionary together.

Patrick relates: "When I was living in the Tokyo area in 1989, I could take a bus to the train station to get into Tokyo. Since I didn't read Japanese, getting the right bus was a problem, until I figured out that the last piece of the name of the station looked like the letter R stretched out a little, and no other bus that came to my stop seemed to have a destination sign that ended that way. The rest of the sign was random doodles with no form or substance to me. But one day, as I became more and more used to the writing, I had an epiphany: I saw a horse next to the stretched R! This came as such a surprise to me I almost didn't get on the bus—after all, since I'd never seen the horse before, this must be a different bus. But it was the right bus, and it turns out the Japanese word for station, eki, is composed of the kanji for horse plus a component that looks like an R." Before there were trains, there were horses, and at stations, they were tied to posts that apparently look like a backward R.

Kiba 騎馬 Horse Riding

Eki 駅 Train Station

Uchi 打 Strike, Chop

Uchi

Uchi can be divided into two halves, left and right. On the left we have a stylized hand, the same one that's in the harai of gedan barai. If you wanted to write Te fast, you might get something like this character, especially if you'd drunk a lot of saké, or caught your own hand in a loom. On the right we see a nail. In a strike our hand nails him. Uchi means 'strike' in English.

5.

The VOID: Taikyoku Yodan

*"Having attained a principle, one detaches from the principle; thus one has spontaneous independence in the science of martial arts and naturally attains marvels: discerning the rhythm when the time comes, one strikes spontaneously and naturally scores."*69
—Miyamoto Musashi, describing Kū (Kara) no Rin, the Ring of The Void

Quintessence

This chapter is the most difficult in *Go Rin no Sho.* Okay, we'll admit we don't fully understand it, but people who have studied it, especially martial artists, say it begins to make sense after much study, or a lot of saké. Let us quote a bit to give you the flavor of this chapter (Patrick's interpretation, but trust us, this interpretation is about the clearest you'll find).

The heart of The Void considers things without form, things that cannot be seen. Certainly, emptiness is what does not exist. To understand existence, you must understand nonexistence. That is The Void. Being in the midst of the world and seeing that which is not, you might think what is incomprehensible is The Void. But this is not The Void—You're just confused. In studying martial arts, students think that what they don't understand is The Void. But it is not the true Void, it's delusion.

Maybe a little *less* saké is needed. Musashi goes on to give what is some valuable advice for anyone studying Martial Arts:

Warriors study Martial Arts carefully and practice diligently. The Way of Warriors is actually easy to understand. With a clear mind, never slacking off, polishing the mind and focusing, sharpening both the eye that sees and the eye that observes, you should know The Void as the state where there is no doubt, and the clouds of confusion dissipate.

89

Taikyoku Yodan Choreography

#	Side	Waza	Technique	Tachi	Notes
1	Left	Gedan Barai	Down Block	Zenkutsu	90° Left Turn
2a	Right	Mae Geri	Front Kick	Zenkutsu	
2b	Right	Oi Zuki	Lunge Punch	Zenkutsu	
2c	Left	Gyaku Zuki	Reverse Punch	Zenkutsu	
3	Right	Gedan Barai	Down Block	Zenkutsu	180° Right Turn
4a	Left	Mae Geri	Front Kick	Zenkutsu	
4b	Left	Oi Zuki	Lunge Punch	Zenkutsu	
4c	Right	Gyaku Zuki	Reverse Punch	Zenkutsu	
5	Left	Gedan Barai	Down Block	Zenkutsu	90° Left Turn
6	Right	Soto Ude Uke	Outside Forearm Block	Kiba	
7	Left	Soto Ude Uke	Outside Forearm Block	Kiba	
8	Right	Soto Ude Uke	Outside Forearm Block	Kiba	**Kiai!**
9	Left	Gedan Barai	Down Block	Zenkutsu	270° Left Turn
10a	Right	Mae Geri	Front Kick	Zenkutsu	
10b	Right	Oi Zuki	Lunge Punch	Zenkutsu	
10c	Left	Gyaku Zuki	Reverse Punch	Zenkutsu	
11	Right	Gedan Barai	Down Block	Zenkutsu	180° Right Turn
12a	Left	Mae Geri	Front Kick	Zenkutsu	
12b	Left	Oi Zuki	Lunge Punch	Zenkutsu	
12c	Right	Gyaku Zuki	Reverse Punch	Zenkutsu	
13	Left	Gedan Barai	Down Block	Zenkutsu	90° Left Turn
14	Right	Soto Ude Uke	Outside Forearm Block	Kiba	Heading Home
15	Left	Soto Ude Uke	Outside Forearm Block	Kiba	
16	Right	Soto Ude Uke	Outside Forearm Block	Kiba	**Kiai!**
17	Left	Gedan Barai	Down Block	Zenkutsu	270° Left Turn
18a	Right	Mae Geri	Front Kick	Zenkutsu	
18b	Right	Oi Zuki	Lunge Punch	Zenkutsu	
18c	Left	Gyaku Zuki	Reverse Punch	Zenkutsu	
19	Right	Gedan Barai	Down Block	Zenkutsu	180° Right Turn
20a	Left	Mae Geri	Front Kick	Zenkutsu	
20b	Left	Oi Zuki	Lunge Punch	Zenkutsu	
20c	Right	Gyaku Zuki	Reverse Punch	Zenkutsu	

See the kata performed at <u>www.wadokikai.com</u>.

Taikyoku Yondan Techniques

Gedan Barai	下段払い	Down Block
Gyaku Zuki	逆突き	Reverse Punch
Kiba Dachi	騎馬立ち	Horse Stance
Mae Geri	前蹴り	Front Kick
Oi Zuki	追い突き	Lunge Punch
Soto Ude Uke	外腕受け	Outside Forearm Block
Yoko Chudan Zuki	横中段突き	Side Middle Punch
Zenkutsu Dachi	前屈立ち	Front Stance

Shinkokata Number 4

From Kamae (Fighting Stance) Mae Geri (Front kick).

Command	Technique	Note
Yōi.	Ready Stance	
Hajime!	Kamae	
(Ichi)	Right Mae Geri	
(Ni)	Left Mae Geri	
(San)	Right Mae Geri	
(Shi)	Left Mae Geri	
(Go)	Right Mae Geri	Kiai!
Kaesu!	Kamae	180° Turn to the Left Counterclockwise
(Ichi)	Right Mae Geri	
(Ni)	Left Mae Geri	
(San)	Right Mae Geri	
(Shi)	Left Mae Geri	
(Go)	Right Mae Geri	Kiai!
Yame.	Ready Stance	

Yondan Technique

Yodan is the last of the Taikyoku Kata. You may say Yodan or Yondan, either is okay, it is entirely your choice. I say tomato, you say tomahto. In the spirit of diversity and eclecticism, and to get you used to both ways, we'll mix it up and use both forms. Yondan has only one new technique, and it's similar to others we've already encountered, so this one isn't too hard to learn. There are two stances, Zenkutsu and Kiba, and our first and only triple combination—a kick, punch, punch—on the wings.

Soto Ude Uke—Outside Forearm Block

Ude Uke is a *Forearm Block*. Unlike the Chudan Ude Uke in Sandan, this block comes from the ear, not the belt. Ude is pronounced like Uday, Saddam Hussein's unfortunate son—ude rhymes with new day.

Training Notes for Soto Ude Uke

- **Keep Low.** Don't lean forward.
- In front, not on the side.

Dojo Lore

Sensei & Sempai

In the movie *The Karate Kid*, the character Mr. Miyagi, having agreed to teach Daniel-San Karate, gives him a seemingly pointless series of chores to perform, such as painting a fence, and waxing some cars, giving him absolutely no instruction in Karate—or so Daniel thinks. Eventually, Daniel becomes frustrated, and decides to quit. Miyagi-Sensei then dramatically reveals that all of the effort was indeed directed toward Karate, as Daniel deftly blocks kicks and punches using the very movements he used to paint the fence and wax the cars. Okay, okay, it's Hollywood, but it's a clever movie, and it does make a certain point about the difference between Japanese and American teaching techniques.

In his book *Autumn Lightning*, Dave Lowry relates how his first lesson in swordsmanship consisted of the teacher, without explanation, repeatedly hitting him, and hard, with a bokken (wooden sword) until he managed to figure out on his own how to dodge it.[70] And Eugen Herrigel's classic *Zen in the Art of Archery* relates how his Master would teach without talk, requiring three years of seemingly undirected groping before he was allowed to actually shoot an arrow at a target![71] Many of the stories and legends of the Martial Arts carry this theme of wordless teaching, forcing students to come to enlightenment unaided by verbal explanations. An Okinawan called Majuro is said to have trained his pupil Sato in a similar way. For over a year, Sato was required to cook and clean, and forbidden to ask any questions about the sword fighting he was there to learn. Then the teacher began attacking him with a tree branch without warning. After a year of these attacks, Sato attained a state of constant, total readiness. Only then did sword training begin, eventually resulting in Sato gaining the nickname 'the unbeatable'.[72] Banzo, the teacher of Matajuro of the famous Yagyū sword clan, summarized the theory concisely. Matajuro was said to have been disowned by his family for his dissolute ways. He convinced Banzo to accept him as a student, but had to cook and clean for three years. Then began the familiar surprise strikes. After a time, Matajuro developed lightning reflexes and was able to sense an approaching attack, becoming an unbeatable sword fighter. Having redeemed himself, he thanked his teacher before taking leave to rejoin his family. But Banzo replied: "I did not teach you anything. The skills you possess were always yours. They were inside you from the beginning. I merely showed you how to let them out."[73]

Sensei is an English word that means *martial arts teacher*. And you thought it was a Japanese word, didn't you? Actually, the English word does come from Japanese, but has undergone revision in its transition into English. The Japanese word literally means *born before*, and so is based on the great Japanese respect for elders, a principle that will gain in merit as you grow older. The term connotes great respect, and applies not just to teachers, but to anyone who is deserving of high esteem for their intellect, such as authors, doctors and scientists. For example, Nobel Prize winners would automatically earn the title, even if they had never taught anything anywhere. As with all Japanese titles, it is gender-neutral. Sensei, San, and Sama apply equally to males and females—Toranaga-Sama, Lord, or Lady, Toranaga. In Japanese, titles follow the name, but as an English word, it usually precedes—we say "Sensei Arce", whereas a Japanese would say "Arce Sensei". It can be applied to either first or last name, so in *The Karate Kid*, Miyagi-Sensei refers to Daniel-San. It can even be attached to a job title. You might say "Omawari-San", Mr. Police Officer—unless you were stopped for speeding, in which case you might try "Omawari-Sama", Lord Police Officer.

In English usage, it simply means *teacher*, but its usage in Japanese is somewhat different. "I am a sensei" if translated directly into Japanese, "Watashi wa sensei desu", would mean "I am an egotistical, conceited person", because since it is a term of great respect, it is considered rude to apply it to yourself. The term is based on your relationship to the individual in question, and endures. For example, a kindergarten teacher who met a highly respected Nobel-Prize-winning professor would certainly refer to the professor as Sensei. Unless, as a child, the professor had been a student of that particular kindergarten teacher, in which case the professor would call the kindergarten teacher Sensei, and not the reverse.

The *sen* in Sensei also appears in Senpai, usually written Sempai to show the consonant shift from N to M. The second character, hai, with a consonant shift to pai, means companion or colleague. The junior in the relationship is the Kōhai, and the two together are Saihai. The term is applied to graduates of the same university, most notably Tokyo University, a Sempai being anyone who graduated in an earlier year. It would be embarrassing to report to a Kohai, so some Japanese companies have actually formed subsidiaries and transferred all the sempai to it before promoting a younger employee to a high-level position, so the Sempai will not technically report to the Kohai. In martial arts, a Sempai would technically mean anyone with a higher belt, but is usually reserved as a term of respect for seniors that have been helpful to you in your training.

Funakoshi's 20 Principles

As authors, we have tremendous respect for Gichin Funakoshi. Like Musashi, he was an accomplished Martial Artist, but he was also a great writer. As we put this book together, we used a number of his quotes, not out of respect, but because they happened to be good. In the 1920s and 30s, Funakoshi developed his Principles of Karate, which will give you some guidance in the ethics of Karate. His first principle deals with Rei, or courtesy. This is the same rei that is used as the command to bow. It is also the rei in Shurei no Mon, the Gate of Courtesy, which is a symbol of Okinawa. The illustration shows the gate as it looked to William Heine, an artist of the Expedition to Japan led by Commodore Matthew C. Perry in the 1850s.[74] Perry used Okinawa as a convenient stopping point during this expedition, which lead to the end of the policy of Sakoku, or closed country, mentioned earlier. The name of Okinawa's archipelago, Ryukyu, was historically written Chinese style, with an L, by Westerners, so expedition *Narrative* refers to Okinawa as Lew Chew.

We will include, without further comment, Funakoshi's Twenty Guiding Principles of Karate, for your contemplation.[75]

1. Karate begins with respect and ends with respect. *Karate-dō wa rei ni hajimari, rei ni owaru koto o wasuruna.*

2. There is no first strike in karate. *Karate ni sente nashi.*

3. Karate assists righteousness. *Karate wa gi no tasuke.*

4. First, know thyself, then know others. *Mazu jiko o shire, shikoshite tao o shire.*

5. Rather than physical technique, mental technique. *Gijutsu yoi shinjutsu.*

6. Let your mind roam freely. *Kokoro wa hanatan koto o yosu.*

7. Calamity springs from carelessness. *Wazawai wa getai ni shozu.*

8. Never think karate is practiced only in the dojo. *Dōjō nomino karate to omou na.*

9. The pursuit of knowledge of Karate takes one's entire life. *Karate no shugyo wa issho de aru.*

10. Everything you encounter is an aspect of Karate; find the marvelous truth there. *Arai-yuru mono o karate-ka seyo, soko ni myo-mi ari.*

11. Karate is like boiling water; if you do not keep the flame high, it turns tepid. *Karate wa yu no goto shi taezu netsudo o ataezareba moto no mizu ni kaeru.*

12. Do not think of winning, think of not losing. *Katsu kangae wa motsu na makenu kangae wa hitsuyo.*

13. Make adjustments according to your opponent. *Tekki ni yotte tenka seyo.*

14. The outcome of a battle depends on how one handles emptiness and fullness (weakness and strength). *Tattakai wa kyo-jitsu no soju ikan ni ari.*

15. Think of a person's hands and feet as swords. *Hito no te ashi o ken to omoe.*

16. When you step beyond your gate, you face a million enemies. *Danshi mon o izureba hyakuman no tekki ari.*

17. Kamae is for beginners; later one stands in shizentai (natural stance). *Kamae wa shoshinsha ni ato wa shizentai.*

18. Perform kata exactly; actual combat is another matter. *Kata wa tadashiku jissen wa betsu mono.*

19. Never forget your own strengths and weaknesses, the limitations of your body, and the relative quality of your techniques. *Chikara no kyojaku; Karada no shinshuku; Waza no kankyu o wasuruna.*

20. Always think and always live the precepts every day. *Tsune ni shinen kufu seyo.*

Yondan Controversy

Multiple Opponents

A common explanation given for a kata is that it is an imaginary fight against multiple opponents. This simplistic explanation might apply to some kata, but probably not to the Taikyoku.

Consider the centerline of a Taikyoku. In each case, the same technique or combination is executed three times in a row. In Taikyoku Sandan, for example, we attack down the centerline with a Yoko Zuki followed by an Uraken Uchi to the opponent's nose. Why do we do it again? One possibility is we missed the first time. If so, we must have also missed the second time because we do it a third time. Does this make sense? You tried a combination twice, and both times it failed. So you try it again? The only other possibility is that there are actually three opponents who each fall for the same trick, conveniently falling to the side, even though struck backward, so you can advance on the next (inattentive) opponent and sucker him with the identical technique.

An alternate explanation for kata is that they are a series of set practices of techniques and combinations, practiced in a certain order, not necessarily to be thought of as against a group of enemies. Elmar Schmeisser, in *Bunkai: Secrets of Karate Kata* says: "Movements were repeated in kata because they were felt to be important, and needed special practice, not that their actual usage required repeated application of the same combination on the same implied attacker."[76] It is probably not helpful, or intended, to try to visualize, say, eight attackers surrounding you before starting a Taikyoku kata. At any one moment, visualize only one opponent at a time.

270 Degrees of Controversy

In each Taikyoku kata, we do two 270 degree turns. Does this make sense? Johnson calls it "The Myth of the 270-Degree Turn". "The Pinan kata of karate, allegedly perfected by the Okinawan Ankho Itosu somewhere between 1905 and 1907, employ 270-degree turns, which are often translated as turns to face and block the attack of another opponent in a multiple-opponent scenario. Why? Even supposing a kata were intended to mimick a fight against multiple opponents, why turn 270 degrees to block the attack of a fresh opponent, when a simple 90-degree turn clockwise would face you in the same direction, and more quickly? Besides, what would the other opponents be doing while you took so much time (in real terms) to turn?"[77]

But it could be razzle-dazzle. The whirling dervishes or the Sumo wrestler's display before a match serves to distract and demoralize the opponent.

Yondan Philosophy

The Void

Tsutomu Ohshima, the translator of Funakoshi's *Kyōhan*, says "Taikyoku is a philosophical term denoting the macrocosm before its differentiation into heaven and earth: hence, chaos or the void."[78] Thus there is a link between Taikyoku and The Void. Guess which character is used for void? That's right! The character for the void is the one and the same kanji that forms the "kara" of Karate.

The word Karate comes from the teaching of Zen, which could be considered to be the backbone of oriental philosophy since ancient times. The Japanese character (kara) means Heaven or Universe, which in addition to containing the heavenly bodies consists of the infinite expanse of empty space. 'Kara' specifically means 'empty' or 'vacant' in Japanese which, in the context of Zen philosophy, relates to human existence as a state of selflessness or nothingness (the state where the self does not exist and all selflessness and selfish thoughts are gone). In other words, man should not be overcome by trifling selfishness, but should seek instead the perfection of his moral character. This is not to be understood in a merely negative sense, however, for, as Lao Tzu teaches, the emptiness of a cup is what makes it useful—"Thus what we gain is something, yet it is by virtue of nothing, that this can be put to use."

This state of selflessness necessitates the desire for people to become just and moral beings. For example, a person should not be motivated by the quest for material wealth and power, should not be envious of others, nor become a burden to society; but live a clean, wholesome, and moral life, with pride and honor no matter what other people say. To be able to attain this state of moral perfection is the ultimate goal of Karate-Dō.

The connection of The Void with Martial Arts goes back a long way. The fifth and final ring of Musashi's *Go Rin no Sho, The Book of Five Rings*, is Kū, an alternate reading for this kanji 'kara'. The difficulty in pinning down its meaning is underscored by the various ways the chapter title has been translated into English. Cleary and Tarver translate it Emptiness. Wilson also translates it Emptiness, but sometimes uses Encompassment. Harris calls it the Void, which is its Esoteric Buddhist connotation. Krause calls it Focus, and Kaufman calls it No-thing. Ochiai simply calls it Kū, that is, he doesn't translate it at all. Kara has a connotation of Quintessence, approaching what Pirsig called Quality in *Zen & the Art of Motorcycle Maintenance*.[79]

Taikyoku And You

"When you do a *Kata* a thousand times you begin to understand the application. When you do a *Kata* five thousand times you begin to see your opponents. When you do a *Kata* ten thousand times those watching you see your opponents."[80]

Funakoshi tells us: "If the twenty movements are to be executed correctly and smoothly, one must practice until these block-attack combinations can be performed in a single continuous motion of breathing and body movement. Through such practice, one will come to understand the three cardinal points of karate, i.e., the light and heavy application of strength, expansion and contraction of the body, and fast and slow techniques. By always practicing the kata seriously and visualizing realistically the opponents around oneself, one will gain insight into the concept that all the movements that shift the body in different directions are equivalent in a higher sense to a single transcendent movement involving the mind, weapon, and body as a unit. Related to this, one will come to understand the statement, "There is no sente [first attack] in karate," the state of absolute passiveness. It is because of these properties that the name Taikyoku has been assigned to these forms."[81]

You will have to make mistakes, and learn from them, if you hope to truly learn Karate. Babe Ruth was the home-run king. He held the Major League record for home runs until Hank Aaron passed him. But many people don't realize he was also the strikeout king. He held the Major League record for strikeouts—until Hank Aaron passed him. The point is you will never achieve greatness if you won't take a chance. This same point is made in *Hagakure: The Book of the Samurai*, by Yamamoto Tsunetomo (translated by William Scott Wilson): "One who has never erred is dangerous".[82]

Karate is learned in three stages, called Shu-Ba-Ri. At first, the student must strictly follow the kata (Shu). Each motion must always be conducted precisely according to the ancient ritual, and one's progress is evaluated based on how faithful one is to the form. Only after mastering the kata are you allowed to alter (Ha, phonetically shifted to Ba) the exact sequences, experiment, and choose your own techniques. Eventually you are allowed to transcend the rules entirely (Ri), and develop your own strategy in complete freedom.

Although Taikyoku is the most basic of our kata, there is quite a lot in it, so you'll have to spend some time perfecting it, even after you've moved on to yellow belt, and even beyond. The approximate amount of time you should expect to spend perfecting these techniques is the rest of your life, unless you try real hard, in which case it will take considerably longer.

Nihongo

The Writing System(s)

The writing system in Japanese makes writing in Japanese the most complicated in the world. Or perhaps, as Jay Rubin says, it's "the world's most clunky writing system".[83] Maybe we should say writing systems, plural, because there are not one, not two, not even three, but *four* writing systems mixed willy-nilly in Japanese text.

Romaji	There is no first strike in karate.	Karate ni sente nashi.
Kanji	漢字	空手に先手なし。
Hiragana	ひらがな	からてにせんてなし。
Katakana	カタカナ	カラテニセンテナシ。

Rōmaji

The good news is you already know one of the writing systems. All Japanese know Rōmaji, based on Roman characters, what look to us like the English alphabet. They're called Romaji because our alphabet actually came from the Romans. Romaji is used by speakers of European languages to spell out Japanese words, but it is also used for abbreviations in Japanese. The telephone company in Japan is called not ATT, but NTT, for Nippon Telephone & Telegraph, using the Roman characters. JR, formerly JNR, is the Japanese National Railway. And JVC is the Japan Victor Company.

Kanji

You've seen a lot of kanji by now, but only the tiniest fraction. There are over 50,000 kanji, so if you want to learn them all, you'd better get started.

Note we had to use some hiragana to make a sentence. Inflections that mark the grammatical function of the word and verb endings are in hiragana. This is how you can tell if text is Chinese or Japanese—It is impossible to write a Japanese sentence without using some hiragana.

Hiragana

The Japanese did improve on Chinese a bit, however, in that they invented a way to represent words phonetically, using simplified versions of Chinese characters. This was an excellent idea, since it allowed Japanese to write out the pronunciation of any Japanese word. In fact, it was such a good idea, they did it twice! There are two parallel systems, hiragana and katakana. Hiragana is used to show the inflections, absent in Chinese, to distinguish multiple pronunciations of the same character, and to write out ideas for which there is no kanji (or that you forgot the kanji for—a not uncommon occurrence, even for natives).

Katakana

Katakana is used to transliterate foreign words into Japanese, so if you learn this system you can read lots of Japanese words, since words in katakana usually came into Japanese from English. If you're going to Japan, learn katakana first, despite the advice you'll receive to learn hiragana first, because there are many English words in Japanese and they're written in katakana.

Katakana is also used for some Okinawan names of kata such as Saifa and Seisan showing they appear foreign to Tokyoites.

Counting

At this point, you're near the end, so you might reward yourself with a few drinks of sake and/or beer, but how to count them? It also works for cups of coffee and bottles of coke, but you usually don't get to count as high, or as flowingly.

Cups & Bottles

Hai is used to count cups, as in cups of saké, and hon, as in the ippon we saw in Chapter 3, is used to count bottles. After about three (cups of saké) you can probably start speaking fluent Japanese without any help. Or at least you'll think you can.

#	Cups	Bottles
1	Ippai	Ippon
2	Nihai	Nihon
3	Sambai	Sambon
4	Yonhai	Shihon
5	Gohai	Gohon
6	Roppai or Rokuhai	Roppon
7	Nanahai	Shichihon or Nanahon
8	Happai or Hachihai	Happon or Hachihon
9	Kyūhai	Kyūhon
10	Jippai	Jippon

Because of the idiosyncratic consonant shifts, *99 Bottles of Beer on the Wall* will be a challenge in Japanese. Sing the song as you drink the bottles. Before long, you will understand the true meaning of The Void.

The End (The Beginning)

I hope that you enjoyed this book and can use some of the information to help you gain balance in your life. Balance is something in life that is so important and is something you should always be aware of to enjoy your life to the fullest.

Watch for more to come from us as we try to write much more interesting data on *Mind Body Spirit*—the Triangle of Life. "In God we trust, everything else must have data".

Beginner's Mind and Shodan

As we mentioned before, 'First Degree' Black Belt is called Shodan, which literally means 'Beginning Level'. Mas Oyama (1923-1994) called his school Kyokushinkai. The Kyoku is indeed the same Kyoku that is in Taikyoku, and the title means Society of the Ultimate Truth. The Kyoku Shin, Ultimate Truth, 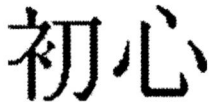 encompasses this observation: "One becomes a beginner after one thousand days of practice and an expert after ten thousand days of practice."[84] If you practice three days a week, you can become a beginner in just six or seven years! But it is not necessarily a bad thing to be a beginner. Shunryu Suzuki of the San Francisco Zen Center wrote a book called *Zen Mind, Beginner's Mind*. Beginner's mind is ShoShin [using the same kanji for *sho* as Shodan, although *shin*'s a different kanji from the Shin of KyokuShin]. Although speaking of Zen, not Karate, he urges us to try to maintain the openness and readiness to learn we have as beginners. "For a while you will keep your beginner's mind, but if you continue to practice one, two, three years or more you are liable to lose the limitless meaning of original mind." Sometimes knowing too much can prevent you from learning more: "If your mind is empty, it is always ready for anything; it is open to everything. In the beginner's mind there are many possibilities, but in the expert's there are few."[85]

By necessity, Patrick has written this with a Beginner's Mind, and Sensei Arce has tried to do so out of conviction. We hope other beginners have benefited, and possibly more advanced students as well. We ask both groups to overlook any errors and accept this meager effort in the spirit it was written. This spirit is best expressed by this statement of the Wadō Ki Kai philosophy:

It is our wish that the ideals of character, sincerity, effort, etiquette, and self-control, as emphasized by Master Funakoshi, and the ultimate goal of moral perfection will enlighten all who train with us and that their lives will be marked by the harmonious interplay of the physical, mental and spiritual aspects of their being.

About the Authors

Patrick McDermott

PATRICK K. McDERMOTT is studying Wadō Ki Kai Karate under Ferol Arce and Grant Butterfield in Alameda, California. He attended Kubasaki Junior High and High Schools in Okinawa, Japan, has a Bachelor of Arts from California State University Sacramento, and a Master of Science from the University of San Francisco. He served in the paddies and in the jungles of Vietnam as a Combat Infantry Sergeant with the 12th Infantry in the199th Light Infantry Brigade of the US Army. He teaches systems analysis at the University of California Berkeley Extension and computer programming at the College of Alameda, and runs his own consulting firm, MCD, Inc., in Oakland, California, specializing in training and consulting on computer technology. pmcdermott@msn.com.

When I was a teenager, I lived in Naha, Okinawa, and had a unique opportunity to study the most famous art of self-defense at its source from the Masters who learned it from their fathers and grandfathers for generations unbroken. Alas, I squandered this golden opportunity, and did not study Karate during my stay in Okinawa. So now, on the wrong side of fifty, I've decided to correct one of the errors and omissions of my misspent youth.

Also by Patrick McDermott:

McDermott, Patrick, *Zen and The Art of Systems Analysis: Meditations on Computer Systems Development*, New York: iUniverse, 2002. ISBNs: 0-595-25679-1 (Paper), 0-595-75230-6 (eBook) & 0-595-65255-7 (Hardback).

Sharp, Alec & Patrick McDermott, *Workflow Modeling: Tools for Process Improvement and Application Development*, Boston: Artech House, 2001. ISBN: 1-58053-021-4.

Ferol Arce

FEROL N. ARCE, 8th Degree Black Belt, has practiced and studied the Martial Arts since 1973. His disciplines include Karate, Ju-Jitsu and weapons. Since 1974 he has concentrated his focus on Karate, originally training under the late John Pereira, Sensei Arce's good friend and teacher.

Born and raised in San Francisco, Arce started his athletic career in baseball, playing for Dante Benedetti. In 1973, he switched to the pursuit of the Art of Karate following a knee injury that prevented him from playing baseball.

Arce obtained his Shodan, or First Degree Black Belt at age 28 in 1978 from Sensei Pereira. According to Arce, he knew early on that he would not only pursue his Martial Arts studies but that he also eventually wanted to teach others the Martial Arts as his way of giving back to the Art.

Encouraged by Sensei Pereira, Arce continued his Wadō Ki Kai training and eventually opened his own dojo, or school, in 1980. He started with just 10 students at the Woman's YWCA in Berkeley, California. By 2003 he had trained thousands of students, awarding Shodan degrees to over 75, and has promoted three to 5th Dan who are teaching WKK Karate and have their own schools in the Bay Area. Arce is currently the head Karate instructor at Mariner Square Athletic Club in Alameda, California, where he has been teaching for over 15 years, and offers classes to students of all levels and backgrounds.

Arce keeps alive the philosophy of Wadō Ki Kai, which means "To Learn From All Things" by sponsoring annual workouts open to other schools and Martial Arts styles. He encourages his students to participate in tournaments and clinics organized by other dojos, and maintains his long standing friendships with ATAMA leaders including Dr. Duke Moore, and Professor Rick Alemany. Both of these men are 10th Dan masters who have been teaching since the 1950s.

A frequent participant in tournaments in his early days, Arce has won in kata & weapons and kumite, weapons being his strongest. He won Grand Champion in the CKC (California Karate Championships) in 1984.

Arce is a member of several major martial arts associations, including ATAMA, and ISOK. In 2001 ATAMA awarded him the prestigious title of Master and presented him with the ceremonial red and white striped belt at the age of 51.

Arce has received the following honors and awards:

> Grand Champion at the CKC
> Teacher of the Year 1984, by ATAMA
> Charter member of I.S.O.K.
> 5th Degree Senior Sensei 1985 by Duke Moore and John Pereira

In 1995 Arce trademarked the Wadō Ki Kai logo. Currently there are 6 Wadō Ki Kai schools in the United States.

Significant Events In Sensei Arce's Career

> 1st Degree Black Belt: 12/2/78, San Francisco, CA
> 5th Degree Black Belt: 1985, San Francisco, CA
> 8th Degree (Master): 2001, Alameda, CA

Arce selflessly passes what he knows on to others. He has an uncanny ability to never ask any more, nor any less, than the student is ready for. (www.wadokikai.com)

About Wadō Ki Kai

和道気会
Wadō Ki Kai
"To Learn from All Things"

The Wadō Ki Kai® system was founded in 1976 by the late John T. Pereira, 8th Degree Black Belt. The English translation means **"To Learn From All Things"**. Practitioners of this style refer to it as "the complete Karate system" due to its incorporation of techniques from other styles in the martial arts. Sensei Pereira was strongly influenced by two of his teachers; Dr. Duke Moore, 10th Degree Black Belt in Karate (a man who also holds Black Belt rank in Judo and Jujitsu), and Richard "Biggie" Kim, another renowned Martial Artist. Kata from the Naha-te, Goju, Shuri-te, and Shoto are all manifest in the Wadō Ki Kai system. Weapons include the Bō, Sai, Tonfa, Nunchaku, and Sword. The adoption of fluid kicking techniques from Tae Kwon Dō is evident when observing Wadō Ki Kai kumite. The most celebrated technique of this style, and one that it is best known for, is the front thrust kick. Sensei Pereira strongly advocated the incorporation of padded sparring equipment in kumite. This idea met with much opposition at the time, but Sensei Pereira nevertheless included it in the Wadō Ki Kai system, and today it is an accepted practice in the Martial Arts world. Today, Master Pereira's unique system of Karate is being taught throughout the Western United States. We that knew him are greatly saddened by his untimely death in 1993, but respectfully share his legacy, and work towards its continuation and growth.

Visit the website at www.wadokikai.com; watch the kata! You'll actually be able to see the kata performed by Sensei Arce, step through it, or stop motion to study any position.

Instructors and Dōjō

Ferol Arce

8th Degree
Head Instructor for Wadō Ki Kai®
arcedo@yahoo.com
Mariner Square Athletic Club
2227 Mariner Square Loop
Alameda, CA 94501
   (510) 523-8011

Alameda, California

Ferol Arce

8th Degree
Head Instructor for Alameda Karate Dō
arcedo@yahoo.com
Mariner Square Athletic Club
2227 Mariner Square Loop
Alameda, CA 94501
    (510) 523-8011

Geoffrey Bradley

5th Degree
Head Instructor for Alameda Kid's Program
Mariner Square Athletic Club
2227 Mariner Square Loop
Alameda, CA 94501
    (510) 523-8011

Grant Butterfield

1st Degree
Head Instructor for Bladium Karate Dō
grant@grantbutterfield.com
The Bladium Sports Club
800 West Tower Avenue Bldg 40
Alameda, CA 94501
    (510) 814-4999

Anthony Corpuz

5th Degree
Head Instructor for Harbor Bay Karate Dō
Harbor Bay Club
200 Packet Landing Rd.
Alameda, CA 94502
    (510) 521-5414

Justin Fawsitt

5th Degree
Shi Han Dai Alameda Karate Dō
Mariner Square Athletic Club
2227 Mariner Square Loop
Alameda, CA 94501
   (510) 523-8011

Contra Costa County, California

Hursey Baker

4th Degree
Head Instructor for San Ramon
24 Hour Fitness
4450 Norris Canyon Rd
San Ramon, CA 94583
   (925) 866-0999

Allen Nunley

4th Degree
Head Instructor Nunley's Karate Dō
Nunley's Karate Do
138 East 3rd St.
Pittsburg, CA 94565
   (925) 473-1275

Santa Fe, New Mexico

Jorge Aigla

6th Degree
Head Instructor for Santa Fe
Saint John's College
Santa Fe, NM 87501-4599
   (505) 984-6000

Solano County, California

Carlos Martinez

6th Degree
Head Instructor Vallejo Karate Dō
Gold's Gym
2425 North Texas Street
Fairfield, CA 94533
   (707) 421-0553

Gold's Gym
848-B Alamo Drive
Vacaville, CA 95688
   (707) 447-0909

Gold's Gym
415 Notre Dame Dr.
Vallejo, CA 94589
   (707) 644-5454

Sources & References

ISBNs starting with 4- are books published in Japan. Many of these are also distributed in the U.S., sometimes under a North American ISBN (0- or 1-). You can also order them from www.amazon.co.jp. You can also order the books in the Japanese language there. Kinokuniya Book stores in San Francisco Japantown ("Nihonmachi") or Los Angeles Little Tokyo ("Ritoru Tōkyō"—*ritoru* is the English *little* pronounced as Japanese) are also great sources. We provided both ISBNs when we had them.

Taikyoku Sources

Your best source to see Taikyoku in action is the Wadō Ki Kai website, www.wadokikai.com.

The following books have pictures of Taikyoku Shodan being performed. We found no source for the other three Taikyoku kata as WKK does them.

Blot, Pierre, *Karate: techniques & tactics*, New York: Sterling Publishing, 2002. ISBN: 0-8069-8217-9. Blot shows pictures of Shodan without any textual explanation.

Funakoshi Gichin, Tsutomu Ohshima, trans., *Karate-dō Kyōhan: The Master Text*, Tokyo: Kodansha International, 1973 (1936), pp. 42-48. ISBNs: 1-87011-190-6 & 4-7700-0370-6. Funakoshi looks at Shodan in detail, pages 42-48. He also discusses Nidan and Sandan, page 47, but they're different from WKK.

Nakamura Tadashi, *Karate: Technique & Spirit*, Boston: Tuttle, 2001, pp. 120-122. ISBN: 0-8048-3282-X. Oyama looks at Shodan in detail, pp. 120-122.

Nakamura Tadashi, Karate: Technique & Spirit, [in Japanese], Tokyo: 2001. ISBN: 4-07-225756-7.

Oyama, Mas, *Karate School*, New York: Sterling Publishing, 2002 (1975), pp. 97-99. ISBN: 0-8069-8897-5. Oyama looks at Shodan in detail, pp. 96-99. He also looks at Sandan in detail, pages 100-103, but it's different from WKK.

Kanji Resources

We used the following references at various times throughout our research.

Karate Kanji

Because of specialized usage and the inherent complexity of the language, identifying the kanji for a given technique is surprisingly difficult. Traditional dictionaries are of limited use. Although they did not cover Taikyoku specifically, these books were especially helpful in finding and confirming the kanji for the various techniques. Errors have surely crept into this work, but there are fewer as a result of these resources.

Funakoshi Gichin, John Teramoto, trans., *Karate Jutsu: The Original Teachings of Master Funakoshi*, Tokyo: Kodansha International, 2001 (1925). ISBN: 4-7700-2681-1.

Japan Karatedo Federation, *Karate Dō Kata Kyōhan: Karatedo Kata Model for Teaching* [Bilingual Japanese/English], Tokyo: Baseball Magazine, 2001. ISBN: 4-583-03645-0.

JTB, *Illustrated Martial Arts & Sports in Japan, Japan in Your Pocket Vol.16*, Tokyo: Japan Travel Bureau, 1993. ISBN: 4-533-0195-1.

Sugiyama, Shojiro & his students, *25 Shōtō-kan Kata, Fifth Edition*, Chicago: J. Toguri Mercantile Company, 2002. ISBN: 0-9669048-0-X. It is not only taiyaku bilingual, it's tri-lingual: the text is in English, Japanese, and Spanish.

Kanji Dictionaries

In addition to standard dictionaries, students of Japanese need a character dictionary to find the meaning and compounds for kanji. There is a health benefit to this, since comprehensive kanji dictionaries are large and bulky, so there is no need to work out with weights—just carry your kanji dictionary around. Both Nelson and S&H have new editions, which is good, since the old editions are still perfectly good, and you can get the books very cheap used ($8-$10). If you want to learn to write the characters, you will need a book that shows the stroke order. Some books list all compounds under each kanji, others only the ones that start with that kanji, and shorter versions only a representative sample.

Halpern, Jack, *NTC's New Japanese-English Character Dictionary*, Lincolnwood, Illinois: National Textbook Company, 1993. ISBN: 0-8442-8434-3. Distinctive Feature: Usage notes, synonyms, homophones. Compounds: A good sampling. Stroke order. An abbreviated version is available under the title *Kanji Learner's Dictionary*.

Halpern, Jack, *The Kodansha Kanji Learner's Dictionary*, Tokyo: Kodansha International, 1999. ISBN: 4-7700-2855-5. Distinctive Feature: Usage notes, synonyms, homophones. Compounds: A good sampling. Stroke order. An abbreviated, and thus more portable, version of *NTC's New Japanese-English Character Dictionary*.

Kodansha, *Kodansha's Pocket Kanji Guide*, Tokyo: Kodansha International, 1994. ISBN: 4-7700-1801-0. Distinctive Feature: Pocket sized (Big Pocket). They mean a cargo pants pocket: Although called "pocket" it will not fit in a normal pocket. Although less comprehensive, this dictionary is more portable.

Nelson, Andrew Nathaniel, *Modern Reader's Japanese-English Character Dictionary, Second Revised Edition*, Rutland, Vermont: Charles E. Tuttle Company, 1962. ISBN: 0-8048-0408-7. Distinctive Feature: Radical Fuzzy Logic. Rather than the historical radicals, a more obvious method is used. If you are interested in the strict historical method, or have masochistic tendencies, you'll want to use a book that uses the historical radicals. Compounds: All Initial, only when the kanji is the first character of the compound. No stroke order. The "Classic" Nelson, not to be confused with The New Nelson.

Nelson, Andrew Nathaniel, John H. Haig, rev., *The New Nelson Japanese-English Character Dictionary*, Rutland, Vermont: Charles E. Tuttle Company, 1997. ISBN: 0-8048-2036-8. Compounds: All Initial. No stroke order. "The New Nelson".

Spahn, Mark & Wolfgang Hadamitzky, *Japanese Character Dictionary: With Compound Lookup via Any Kanji*, Tokyo: Nichigai Associates, Inc., 1989. ISBN: 4-8169-0828-5. Distinctive Feature: All compounds in all listings. Interestingly enough, translated into English from the original German! Old version of *The Kanji Dictionary*.

Spahn, Mark & Wolfgang Hadamitzky, *The Kanji Dictionary*, Boston: Tuttle Publishing, 1996. ISBN: 1-8048-2058-9. Compounds: All compounds in all listings. No stroke order. Translated into English from the original German. New version of *Japanese Character Dictionary*.

Kanji Learning Systems

Although easier to learn if you stick with it to the end, a system makes the book less desirable as a reference book. It is also less useful for an eclectic or serendipitous learner, so if you are specifically interested in, say, Martial Arts, it doesn't work as well since the explanation for a kanji builds on previous kanji you might not have learned. We nonetheless consult these books from time to time, and you'll probably want to get one of these if you want to learn the writing system.

Dykstra, Andrew, *The Kanji ABC*, Honolulu: Kanji Press, 1987. ISBN: 0-917880-00-5. Dykstra, Andrew, *Kanji 1-2-3*, Honolulu: Kanji Press, 1987. ISBN: 0-917880-01-3. Dykstra, Andrew, *Kanji Ichi Ni*, Honolulu: Kanji Press, 1992. ISBN: 0-917880-02-1. Compounds: No. Stroke order. Fun little books. Not meant to be comprehensive.

Hadamitzky, Wolfgang & Mark Spahn, *Kana & Kanji: A Handbook and Dictionary Japanese Writing System*, Rutland, Vermont: Charles E. Tuttle, 1981. ISBN: 0-8048-1373-6. Compounds: A half dozen or so, pedagogically. Stroke order. Translated into English from the original German!

Heisig, James W., *Remembering the Kanji I: a complete course on how not to forget the meaning and writing of Japanese characters*, Tokyo: Japan Publications Trading Company, 1977. ISBN: 0-87040-739-2. Heisig, James W., *Remembering the Kanji II: a Systematic Guide to Reading Japanese characters*, Tokyo: Japan Publications Trading Company, 2001. ISBN: 0-87040-748-1. Heisig, James W., *Remembering the Kanji III: writing and Reading Japanese characters for Upper-Level Proficiency*, Tokyo: Japan Publications Trading Company, 2001. ISBN: 0-87040-931-X. Volume I teaches the character's meaning in English; Volume II the Japanese readings; Volume III more advanced. Compounds: None. No stroke order.

Henshall, Kenneth G., *A Guide to Remembering Japanese Characters*, Rutland, Vermont: Charles E. Tuttle, 1988. ISBN: 0-8048-1532-1. Compounds: None. No stroke order.

O'Neill, P.G., *Essential Kanji: 2,000 Basic Japanese Characters Systematically Arranged for Learning and Reference*, New York: Weatherhill, 1973. ISBN: 0-8348-0222-8. Compounds: A half dozen or so, pedagogically. Stroke order.

References

These are reference source notes for the text.

CHAPTER 1 Ground—The Taikyoku Reference Notes

Note 1: Funakoshi Gichin, Tsutomu Ohshima, trans., *Karate-dō Kyōhan: The Master Text*, Tokyo: Kodansha International, 1973 (1936), p 9. ISBNs: 0-87011-190-6 & 4-7700-0370-6.

Note 2: Funakoshi Gichin, Tsutomu Ohshima, trans., *Karate-dō Kyōhan: The Master Text*, Tokyo: Kodansha International, 1973 (1936), p. 35. ISBNs: 0-87011-190-6 & 4-7700-0370-6.

Note 3: McCarthy, Pat, *Classical Kata of Okinawan Karate*, Santa Clarita, California: Ohara Publications, 1987, p. 61. ISBN: 0-89750-113-6.

Note 4: Grupp, Joachim, James Beachus, trans., *Shotokan Karate Kata, Vol. 1*, Aachen: Meyer & Meyer Sport, 2002, p. 19. ISBN 1-84126-088-6.

Note 5: Ohshima Tsutomu, *Notes on Training*, Ravensdale, Washington: Pine Winds Press, 1998, p. 10. ISBN: 0-937663-32-8.

Note 6: Blot, Pierre, *Karate: techniques & tactics*, New York: Sterling Publishing, 2002, p. 50. ISBN: 0-8069-8217-9.

Note 7: Your best source to see Taikyoku in action is the Wadō Ki Kai website, www.wadokikai.com. Our other sources were: Blot, Pierre, *Karate: techniques & tactics*, New York: Sterling Publishing, 2002. ISBN: 0-8069-8217-9. Funakoshi Gichin, Tsutomu Ohshima, trans., *Karate-dō Kyōhan: The Master Text*, Tokyo: Kodansha International, 1973 (1936), pp. 42-48. ISBNs: 1-87011-190-6 & 4-7700-0370-6. Nakamura Tadashi, *Karate: Technique & Spirit*, Boston: Tuttle, 2001, pp. 120-122. ISBN: 0-8048-3282-X. Nakamura Tadashi, Karate: Technique & Spirit, [in Japanese], Tokyo: 2001. ISBN: 4-07-225756-7. Oyama, Mas, *Karate School*, New York: Sterling Publishing, 2002 (1975), pp. 97-99. ISBN: 0-8069-8897-5. Oyama looks at Shodan in detail, pp. 96-99.

Note 8: Lee, Bruce, *The Tao of Jeet Kune Do*, Santa Clarita, California: Ohara Publications, 1975. ISBN: 0-89750-048-2.

Note 9: Seward, Jack, *Japanese in Action: An Unorthodox Approach to the Spoken Language and the People Who Speak It (Revised Edition)*, New York: Weatherhill, 1968. p. 28. ISBN: 0-8348-0033-0.

Note 10: Funakoshi Gichin, Tsutomu Ohshima, trans., *Karate-dō Kyōhan: The Master Text*, Tokyo: Kodansha International, 1973 (1936), pp. 47-48. ISBNs: 0-87011-190-6 & 4-7700-0370-6.

Note 11: Hsu, Feng-Hsiung, *Behind Deep Blue: Building the Computer that Defeated the World Chess Champion*, Princeton, New Jersey: Princeton University Press, 2002, p. 272. ISBN: 0-691-09065-3.

Note 12: Funakoshi Gichin, Tsutomu Ohshima, trans., *Karate-dō Kyōhan: The Master Text*, Tokyo: Kodansha International, 1973 (1936), p. 37. ISBNs: 0-87011-190-6 & 4-7700-0370-6.

Note 13: Yamaguchi, N. Gosei, *Goju-Ryu Karate II*, San Francisco: Goju-Kai Karate-Do USA, 1999 (1974), p. 133. ISBN: 0-9672821-1-X.

Note 14: Nagamine Shoshin, *The Essence of Okinawan Karate-Do*, Boston: Tuttle Publishing, 1976, p. 104. ISBN: 0-8048-2110-0.

Note 15: Yamaguchi, N. Gosei, *Goju-Ryu Karate II*, San Francisco: Goju-Kai Karate-Do USA, 1999 (1974), p. 133. ISBN: 0-9672821-1-X.

Note 16: Ohshima Tsutomu, *Notes on Training*, Ravensdale, Washington: Pine Winds Press, 1998, p. 10. ISBN: 0-937663-32-8.

Note 17: Nakamura Tadashi, *Karate: Technique & Spirit*, Boston: Tuttle, 2001, p. 118. ISBN: 0-8048-3282-X.

Note 18: Adrogué, Manuel E., "Ancient Military Manuals and their Relation to Modern Korean Martial Arts", in *Journal of Asian Martial Arts*, Vol 12, No. 3, 2003, p. 31. ISSN: 1057-8358.

Note 19: Funakoshi Gichin & Genwa Nakasone, John Teramoto, trans., *The Twenty Guiding Principles of Karate: The Spiritual Legacy of the Master*, Tokyo: Kodansha International, 2003 (1938), p. 125. ISBN: 4-7700-2796-6.

Note 20: Suzuki, Daisetz T., *Zen and Japanese Culture*, New York: MJF Books, 1959, p. 176. ISBN: 1-56731-124-5.

Note 21: Miyamoto Musashi, Thomas Cleary, trans., *The Book of Five Rings*, Boston: Shambhala Pocket Classics, 1994 (1643). ISBN: 0-87773-998-6.

Note 22: Translation of Principles 1 & 9 from Miyamoto Musashi, Thomas Cleary, trans., *The Book of Five Rings*, Boston: Shambhala, 1993 (1643). ISBN: 1-57062-748-7. Translation of Principles 2 & 8 from Miyamoto Musashi, Victor Harris, trans., *A Book of Five Rings*, Woodstock, New York: The Overlook Press, 1974 (1643). ISBN: 0-87951-018-8. Translation of Principles 3 & 7 from Nihon Services Corporation, *The Book of Five Rings: The Real Art of Japanese Management*, Toronto: Bantam Books, 1982. Translation of Principle 4 from Miyamoto Musashi, William Scott Wilson, trans., *The Book of Five Rings*, Tokyo: Kodansha International, 2002. Translation of Principle 5 by Patrick McDermott, based on Miyamoto Musashi, Kamata Shigeo, trans. [into modern Japanese] *Go Rin no Sho* [in olde and modern Japanese], Tokyo: Kodansha Gakusho Bunko, 1986 (1643). ISBN: 4-06-158735-8; and Miyamoto Musashi, Watanabe Ichirō, trans. [into modern Japanese] *Go Rin no Sho* [in olde and modern Japanese], Tokyo: Iwanami Shoten, 1985 (1643). ISBN: 4-00-330021-1. Translation of Principle 6 from Miyamoto Musashi, D. E. Tarver, trans., *The Book of Five Rings*, San Jose: Writers Club Press, 2002 (1643). ISBN: 0-595-23006-7.

Note 23: Seward, Jack, *Japanese in Action: An Unorthodox Approach to the Spoken Language and the People Who Speak It (Revised Edition)*, New York: Weatherhill, 1968, p. 9. ISBN: 0-8348-0033-0.

Note 24: Murray, D.M. & T.W. Wong, *Noodle Words: an introduction to Chinese and Japanese characters*, Rutland, Vermont: Charles E. Tuttle, 1971. ISBN: 0-8048-0948-8.

Note 25: The allusion is to Chamberlain, Basil Hall, *Japanese Things: Being Notes on Various Subjects Connected with Japan*, Rutland, Vermont: Charles E. Tuttle Company, 1971 (originally *Things Japanese*, 1905). ISBN: 0-8048-0713-2.

CHAPTER 2 Water—Taikyoku Shodan Reference Notes

Note 26: Reilly, Robin L., *Complete Shotokan Karate: History, Philosophy, and Practice; The Samurai Legacy and Modern Practice*, Boston: Charles E. Tuttle, 1985, p. 89. ISBN: 0-8048-2108-9.

Note 27: Lee, Bruce, John Little, ed., *The Tao of Gung Fu: A Study in the Way of Chinese Martial Art*, Boston: Tuttle Publishing, 1997, p. 138. ISBN: 0-8048-3110-6. Bruce recites this paragraph in Heller, Paul, "Bruce Lee in his Own Words"on the DVD *Enter the Dragon: Special Edition*, Burbank: Warner Brothers, 1998.

Note 28: Funakoshi Gichin, Tsutomu Ohshima, trans., *Karate-dō Kyōhan: The Master Text*, Tokyo: Kodansha International, 1973 (1936), p. 42. ISBNs: 0-87011-190-6 & 4-7700-0370-6.

Note 29: Nakamura Tadashi, *Karate: Technique & Spirit*, Boston: Tuttle, 2001, p. 120. ISBN: 0-8048-3282-X.

Note 30: Ohshima Tsutomu, *Notes on Training*, Ravensdale, Washington: Pine Winds Press, 1998, p. 10. ISBN: 0-937663-32-8.

Note 31: Funakoshi Gichin, John Teramoto, trans., *Karate Jutsu: The Original Teachings of Master Funakoshi*, Tokyo: Kodansha International, 2001 (1925), p. 51. ISBN: 4-7700-2681-1.

Note 32: Sugiyama, Shojiro & his students, *25 Shōtō-kan Kata, Fifth Edition* [Tri-lingual Japanese/English/Spanish], Chicago: J. Toguri Mercantile Company, 2002, p. 53. ISBN: 0-9669048-0-X.

Note 33: Patrick McDermott's interpretation. This translation, like all of Patrick's translations of Musashi, is based on Miyamoto Musashi, Watanabe Ichirō, trans. [into modern Japanese] *Go Rin no Sho* [in olde and modern Japanese], Tokyo: Iwanami Shoten, 1985 (1643). ISBN: 4-00-330021-1. Miyamoto Musashi, Kamata Shigeo, trans. [into modern Japanese] *Go Rin no Sho* [in olde and modern Japanese], Tokyo: Kodansha Gakusho Bunko, 1986 (1643). ISBN: 4-06-158735-8.

Note 34: See, for example, Funakoshi Gichin, John Teramoto, trans., *Karate Jutsu: The Original Teachings of Master Funakoshi*, Tokyo: Kodansha International, 2001 (1925), pp. 60, 70, 71, 85, etc. ISBN: 4-7700-2681-1.

Note 35: Nagamine Shoshin, *The Essence of Okinawan Karate-Do*, Boston: Tuttle Publishing, 1976, p. 45. ISBN: 0-8048-2110-0. Nagamine holds his fist high, see pictures pp. 70,16, 75, 84, etc.

Note 36: Blot, Pierre, *Karate: techniques & tactics*, New York: Sterling Publishing, 2002. ISBN: 0-8069-8217-9. Funakoshi Gichin, Tsutomu Ohshima, trans., *Karate-dō Kyōhan: The Master Text*, Tokyo: Kodansha International, 1973 (1936), pp. 42-48. ISBNs: 1-87011-190-6 & 4-7700-0370-6. Nakamura Tadashi, *Karate: Technique & Spirit*, Boston: Tuttle, 2001, pp. 120-122. ISBN: 0-8048-3282-X—the English release of Nakamura Tadashi, *Karate: Technique & Spirit*, [in Japanese], Tokyo: 2001. ISBN: 4-07-225756-7. Oyama, Mas, *Karate School*, New York: Sterling Publishing, 2002 (1975), pp. 97-99. ISBN: 0-8069-8897-5.

Note 37: Yamaguchi, N. Gosei, *Goju-Ryu Karate II*, San Francisco: Goju-Kai Karate-Do USA, 1999 (1974), pp. 217-243. ISBN: 0-9672821-1-X.

Note 38: Clark, *Rick, 75 Down Blocks: Refining Karate Technique*, Boston: Tuttle Publishing, 2003. ISBN: 0-8048-3218-8.

Note 39: Nicol, C.W., *Moving Zen: Karate As a Way to Gentleness*, New York: Quill, 1982, p. 45. ISBN: 0-688-01181-0.

Note 40: Kanazawa Hirokaze, *Karate: Roku Shūkan* [in Japanese], Tokyo: 2000. ISBN: 4-89224-742-1.

Note 41: Funakoshi Gichin, Shingo Ishida, trans., *To-Te Jitsu*, Hamilton, Ontario: Masters Publication, 1997 (1922). ISBN: 0-920129-22-6.

Note 42: Spahn, Mark & Wolfgang Hadamitzky, *The Kanji Dictionary*, Boston: Tuttle Publishing, 1996, p. 829. ISBNs: 1-8048-2058-9; 4-8053-0545-2.

Note 43: Nelson, Andrew Nathaniel, *Modern Reader's Japanese-English Character Dictionary, Second Revised Edition*, Rutland, Vermont: Charles E. Tuttle Company, 1962, p. 672. ISBN: 0-8048-0408-7. Nelson, Andrew Nathaniel, John H. Haig, rev., *The New Nelson Japanese-English Character Dictionary*, Rutland, Vermont: Charles E. Tuttle Company, 1997, p. 816. ISBN: 0-8048-2036-8.

Note 44: McCarthy, Patrick, comm. & trans., *Ancient Okinawan Martial Arts, Volume 2: Koryu Uchinadi*, Boston: Tuttle Publishing, 1999, pp. 60-61. ISBN: 0-8048-3147-5.

Note 45: Lerner, Alan Jay, *My Fair Lady*, New York: Signet Classics, 1969 (1956), p. 135.

Note 46: Henshall, Kenneth G., *A Guide to Remembering Japanese Characters*, Rutland, Vermont: Charles E. Tuttle, 1988, Index 350, p. 105. ISBN: 0-8048-1532-1.

CHAPTER 3 Fire—Taikyoku Nidan Reference Notes

Note 47: Miyamoto Musashi, William Scott Wilson & Michihiro Matsumoto, trans., *Taiyaku* [Bilingual Japanese/English] *Go Rin Sho: The Book of Five Rings*, Tokyo: Kodansha International, 2001, p. 57. ISBN: 4-7700-2844-X.

Note 48: Nicol, C.W., *Moving Zen: Karate As a Way to Gentleness*, New York: Quill, 1982 (1975), pp. 29-30. ISBN: 0-688-01181-0. Reissued as Nicol, C.W., *Moving Zen: One Man's Journey to the Heart of Karate*, Tokyo: Kodansha International, 2001 (1975), p. 40. ISBN: 4-7700-2755-9.

Note 49: Funakoshi Gichin, Tsutomu Ohshima, trans., *Karate-dō Kyōhan: The Master Text*, Tokyo: Kodansha International, 1973 (1936), p. 47. ISBNs: 0-87011-190-6 & 4-7700-0370-6.

Note 50: Schmeisser, Elmar T. Ph.D., *Bunkai: Secrets of Karate, Volume 1: The Tekki Series*, St. Charles, Missouri: Damashi, 1999, p. 13. ISBN: 0-911921-36-2.

Note 51: Nakayama, Masatoshi, *Dynamic Karate: Instruction by the Master*, Tokyo: Kodansha International, 1986 (1966), p. 192. ISBNs: 0-87011-788-2 & 4-7700-1288-8.

Note 52: Burgar, Bill, *Five Years, One Kata: Putting kata back at the heart of karate*, UK: Martial Arts Publishing, 2003, pp. 110-112. ISBN: 0-9544466-0-7.

Note 53: Lee, Bruce, *Chinese Gung Fu: The Philosophical Art of Self-Defense*, Santa Clarita, California: Ohara Publications, 1963, p. 81. ISBN: 0-89750-112-8.

CHAPTER 4 Wind—Taikyoku Sandan Reference Notes

Note 54: Miyamoto Musashi, Thomas Cleary, trans., *The Book of Five Rings*, Boston: Shambhala Pocket Classics, 1994 (1643), p. 115. ISBN: 0-87773-998-6.

Note 55: Lederer, Richard, *Crazy English: The Ultimate Joy Ride Through Our Language*, New York: Pocket Books, 1989, p. 23. ISBN: 0-671-68907-X.

126 • Karate's Supreme Ultimate

Note 56: Funakoshi Gichin, *Karate-dō: My Way of Life*, Tokyo: Kodansha International, 1975 (1956), p. 106. ISBN: 0-87011-463-8.

Note 57: Funakoshi Gichin, *Karate-dō: My Way of Life*, Tokyo: Kodansha International, 1975 (1956), p. 46-47. ISBN: 0-87011-463-8.

Note 58: References for Sandan were: Oyama, Mas, *Karate School*, New York: Sterling Publishing, 2002 (1975). ISBN: 0-8069-8897-5.Funakoshi Gichin, Tsutomu Ohshima, trans., Karate-dō Kyōhan: The Master Text, Tokyo: Kodansha International, 1973 (1936), p. 47. ISBNs: 0-87011-190-6 & 4-7700-0370-6. And Nakamura Tadashi, *Karate: Technique & Spirit*, [in Japanese], Tokyo: 2001. ISBN: 4-07-225756-7.

Note 59: Funakoshi Gichin, Tsutomu Ohshima, trans., *Karate-dō Kyōhan: The Master Text*, Tokyo: Kodansha International, 1973 (1936), p. 42-48. ISBNs: 0-87011-190-6 & 4-7700-0370-6.

Note 60: Funakoshi Gichin, Tsutomu Ohshima, trans., *Karate-dō Kyōhan: The Master Text*, Tokyo: Kodansha International, 1973 (1936), p. 47. ISBNs: 0-87011-190-6 & 4-7700-0370-6.

Note 61: Funakoshi Gichin, *Karate-dō: My Way of Life*, Tokyo: Kodansha International, 1975 (1956), p. 1. ISBN: 0-87011-463-8.

Note 62: Ochiai, Hidy, *A Way to Victory: The Annotated Book of Five Rings*, Woodstock, New York: The Overlook Press, 2001, p. 16. ISBN: 1-58567-038-3.

Note 63: Okakura, Kakuzo, *The Book of Tea*, New York: Dover Publications, 1964 (1906). ISBN: 0-486-20070-1.

Note 64: Lao-tzu, Stephen Mitchell, trans., *Tao Te Ching*, New York: HarperPerennial, 1988 (~500 b.c.e), Chapter 1, p. 1. ISBN: 0-06-081245-1.

Note 65: McDermott, Patrick, *Zen & The Art of Systems Analysis: Meditations on Computer Systems Development*, New York: iUniverse, 2002, p. 114-115. ISBNs: 0-595-25679-1 (Paper), 0-595-75230-6 (eBook) & 0-595-65255-7 (Hardback).

Note 66: Nitobe, Inazo, *Bushido: The Soul of Japan*, Boston: Tuttle Publishing, 2001 (1899), p. 15.

Note 67: Musashi, Miyamoto, Thomas Cleary, trans., *The Book of Five Rings*, Boston: Shambhala Pocket Classics, 1994 (1643), p. xx.

Note 68: Suzuki Takao, Akira Miura, trans., *Words in Context: A Japanese Perspective on Language and Culture*, Tokyo: Kodansha International, 1978. ISBNs: 0-87011-642-8; 4-7700-1142-3.

CHAPTER 5 The Void—Taikyoku Yondan Reference Notes

Note 69: Miyamoto Musashi, Thomas Cleary, trans., *The Book of Five Rings*, Boston: Shambhala Pocket Classics, 1994 (1643), p. 19-20. ISBN: 0-87773-998-6.

Note 70: Lowry, Dave, *Autumn Lightning: The Education of an American Samurai*, Boston: Shambhala, 2001, pp. 22-24. ISBN: 1-57062-115-2.

Note 71: Herrigel, Eugen, R.F.C. Hull, trans., *Zen in the Art of Archery*, New York: Vintage Books, 1953. ISBN: 0-375-70509-0.

Note 72: Lewis, Peter, *Myths and Legends of the Martial Arts: Origins, Philosophy, Practice*, London: Prion Books, 1998, pp. 109-112. ISBN: 1-85375-271-1.

Note 73: Kimmel, Eric A., *Sword of the Samurai: Adventure Stories from Japan*, New York: HarperTrophy, 1999, p. 40. ISBN: 0-06-442131-7.

Note 74: Perry, Commodore M.C., *Narrative of the Expedition of an American Squadron to the China Seas and Japan*, Washington, D.C.: Congress of the United States, 1856. Available in reprint as Perry, Commodore M.C., *Narrative of the Expedition to the China Seas and Japan, 1852-1855*, Mineola, New York: Dover Publications, 2000, (1856). ISBN: 0-486-41133-8. The plate shown faces page 188.

Note 75: Translation of Principles 1 & 20 from Kim, Richard, *The Classical Man*, Hamilton, Ontario: Masters Publication, 1982, pp. 103-105. ISBN: 0-920129-01-3. Translation of Principles 2, 7, 13, 14, 16, 17 & 18 from Funakoshi Gichin & Genwa Nakasone, John Teramoto, trans., *The Twenty Guiding Principles of Karate: The Spiritual Legacy of the Master*, Tokyo: Kodansha International, 2003 (1938). ISBN: 4-7700-2796-6. Translation of Principles 3, 4, 9, 12 & 15 by Patrick McDermott. Translation of Principles 5, 6, 10, and 19 from Stevens, John, *Budo Secrets: Teachings of the Martial Arts Masters*, Boston: Shambhala, 2002, pp 24-25. ISBN: 1-57062-915-3. Translation of Principles 8 & 11 from *Stevens, John, Three Budo Masters: Jigoro Kano (Judo); Gichin Funakoshi (Karate); Morihei Ueshiba (Aikido)*, Tokyo: Kodansha International, 1995, pp. 82-85. ISBN: 4-7700-1852-5.

Note 76: Schmeisser, Elmar T. Ph.D., *Bunkai: Secrets of Karate, Volume 1: The Tekki Series*, St. Charles, Missouri: Damashi, 1999, pp. 12-13. ISBN: 0-911921-36-2.

Note 77: Johnson, Nathan J., *Barefoot Zen: the Shaolin roots of Kung Fu and Karate*, York Beach, Maine: Samuel Weiser, 2000, p. 119. ISBN: 1-57863-142-4.

Note 78: Funakoshi Gichin, Tsutomu Ohshima, trans., *Karate-dō Kyōhan: The Master Text*, Tokyo: Kodansha International, 1973 (1936), translator's note, p. 42. ISBNs: 1-87011-190-6 & 4-7700-0370-6.

Note 79: Pirsig, Robert, *Zen and the Art of Motorcycle Maintenance: An Inquiry into Values*, New York: Bantam Books, 1974. ISBN: 0-688-00230-7.

Note 80: Frost, Brian, *Koei-Kan Karate-Do: Practice and Precept*, Berkeley: Frog, Ltd., 1998, p. 65. ISBN: 1-883319-64-1.

Note 81: Funakoshi Gichin, Tsutomu Ohshima, trans., *Karate-dō Kyōhan: The Master Text*, Tokyo: Kodansha International, 1973 (1936), p. 48. ISBNs: 0-87011-190-6 & 4-7700-0370-6.

Note 82: Yamamoto Tsunetomo, William Scott Wilson, trans., *Hagakure: The Book of the Samurai*, Tokyo: Kodansha International, 1979 (1716). ISBN: 4-7700-1106-7.

Note 83: Rubin, Jay, *Making Sense of Japanese: What the Textbooks Don't Tell You*, Tokyo: Kodansha International, 1998, p. 93. ISBN: 4-7700-2902-4.

EPILOG Reference Notes

Note 84: Lorden, Michael J., *Oyama: The Legend, The Legacy*, Burbank, California: Multi-Media Books, 2000, p. 48. ISBN: 1-892515-24-5.

Note 85: Suzuki Shunryu, *Zen Mind, Beginner's Mind*, New York: Weatherhill, 1970, p. 21. ISBN: 0-8348-0079-9.

Glossary of Japanese Terms

AGE UKE Rising Block.

AGE ZUKI Rising Punch.

AIUCHI "Simultaneous Scoring Technique." No point awarded to either contestant. Referee brings fists together in front of the chest.

AKA, AKAI Red

AKA (SHIRO) NO KACHI "Red (White) Wins!" The Referee obliquely raises his arm on the side of the winner.

AKA (SHIRO) IPPON "Red (White) Scores Ippon." The Referee obliquely raises his arm on the side of the winner (as in…NO KACHI).

ASHI BARAI Foot Sweep.

ASHI WAZA Name given to leg and foot techniques.

ATAMA American Teachers Association of the Martial Arts.

ATEMI WAZA Striking techniques that are normally used in conjunction with grappling and throwing techniques.

ATENAI YONI "Warning without penalty." This may be imposed for attended minor infractions or for the first instance of a minor infraction. The Referee raises one hand in a fist with the other hand covering it at chest level and shows it to the offender.

ATOSHI BARAKU "A little more time left." An audible signal will be given by the timekeeper 30 seconds before the actual end of the bout.

ATTATE IRU "Contact".

AWASE UKE Joined Hand Block.

AWASE ZUKI U Punch. Also referred to as MOROTE ZUKI.

AYUMI DACHI A stance found in ITOSU-KAI SHITO-RYU. It is a natural "Walking" stance with the weight over the center.

BARAI Combining form of Harai, Sweep.

BASSAI Alternate transliteration of Kata POTSAI.

BŌ Staff. A long stick used as a weapon (approximately 6 feet long).

BUDŌ Martial Arts. "Martial way". The Japanese character for "BU" (martial) is derived from characters meaning "stop" and (a weapon like a) "halberd." In conjunction, then, "BU" may have the connotation "to stop the halberd." In Karate, there is an assumption that the best way to prevent violent conflict is to emphasize the cultivation of individual character. The way (DO) of Karate is thus equivalent to the way of BU, taken in this sense of preventing or avoiding violence so far as possible.

BUDŌKA A practitioner of the Martial Arts, such as a KARATEKA or JŪDŌKA.

BUNKAI A study of the techniques and applications in KATA.

CHINTŌ A kata studied by Blue Belts in WKK. Some claim Chinto is a Chinese martial artist's name. The Shotokan's name for this kata is Gankaku.

CHOKU ZUKI Straight Punch.

CHŪDAN Mid-section. During the practice of KIHON IPPON KUMITE (one step basic sparring), the attacker will normally announce whether the attack will be JODAN, CHUDAN, or GEDAN (Upper level, Midlevel, or Lower level).

CHŪDAN ZUKI A punch to the mid-section of the opponent's body.

CHUI "Warning".

DACHI Combining form of Tachi, Stance.

DAI Attached to the name of a kata, the original, i.e not the variation. It literally means Big, Greater or Major.

DAN Lever, Rank or Degree. Black Belt rank. Ranks under Black Belt are called KYŪ.

DŌ Way/path. The Japanese character for "DO" is the same as the Chinese character for Tao (as in "Taoism"). In Karate, the connotation is that of a way of attaining enlightenment or a way of improving one's character through traditional training.

DŌJŌ Literally "place of the Way." Also "place of enlightenment." The place where we practice Karate. Traditional etiquette prescribes bowing in the direction of the designated front of the dojo (SHOMEN) whenever entering or leaving the dojo.

DŌMŌ ARIGATO GOZAIMASHITA (or GOZAIMASU) Japanese for "thank you very much." At the end of each class, it is proper to bow and thank the instructor and those with whom you've trained. Less formally, Arigato, or Domo Arigato.

DZUKI Combining form of Tsuki, Punch.

EKKU A wooden oar used by the Okinawans which was improvised as a weapon.

EMBUSEN Floor pattern of a given kata.

EMPI (1) A kata studied by Purple Belts in WKK. "The Dancing Sparrow". This kata is the sister kata to Suparenpei, the most advanced kata in Naha-Te.

EMPI (2) Elbow. Sometimes referred to as HIJI.

EMPI UCHI Elbow strike (also called HIJI-ATE)

ENCHO-SEN "Extension." After a draw, the match goes into overtime. Referee reopens match with command "SHOBU HAJIME."

FUDŌ DACHI Immovable Stance. Also referred to as SOCHIN DACHI.

FUJUBUN "Not enough power"

FUKUSHIN SHUGO "Judges Conference".

FUMIKOMI Stomp kick, usually applied to the knee, shin, or instep of an opponent.

GANKAKU The Shotokan's name for Kata CHINTŌ. "Crane on Rock".

GANKAKU DACHI Crane Stance, sometimes referred to as TSURU ASHI DACHI and SAGI ASHI DACHI.

GASSHUKUA special training camp.

GEDAN Lower section. During the practice of KIHON IPPON KUMITE (one step basic sparring), the attacker will normally announce where he/she will attack JODAN, CHUDAN, or GEDAN (Upper level, Midlevel, or Lower level).

GEDAN BARAI Down Block.

GEDAN UDE UKE Low Forearm Block.

GEDAN ZUKI A punch to the lower section of the opponent's body.

GERI Combining form of Keri, Kick.

GI (DO GI) (KEIKO GI) (KARATE GI) Training uniform. In WKK and in most other traditional Japanese and Okinawan Karate Dojo, the GI is white and cotton (synthetics with cotton allowed).

GO NO SEN The tactic where one allows the opponent to attack first to open up targets for counterattack.

GOHON KUMITE Five step basic sparring. The attacker steps in five consecutive times with a striking technique with each step. The defender steps back five times, blocking each technique. After the fifth block, the defender executes a counter-strike.

GYAKU MAWASHI GERI Reverse Roundhouse Kick.

GYAKU ZUKI Reverse Punch.

HACHIJI DACHI A natural stance, feet positioned about one shoulder width apart, with feet pointed slightly outward.

HAI "Yes".

HAISHU UCHI A strike with the back of the hand.

HAISHU UKE A block using the back of the hand.

HAITŌ UCHI Ridge-hand Strike.

HAJIME "Begin". A command given to start a given drill, kata, or kumite.

HANGETSU The Shotokan's name for Kata SEISAN. "Half Moon".

HANGETSU DACHI "Half-Moon" Stance.

HANSHI "Master." An honorary title given to the highest Black Belt of an organization, signifying their understanding of their Art.

HANSOKU "Foul." This is imposed following a very serious infraction. It results in the opponent's score being raised to SANBON. HANSOKU is also invoked when the number of HANSOKU-CHUI and KEIKOKU imposed raise the opponent's score to SANBON. The Referee points with an index finger to the face of the offender at a 45 degree angle and announces a victory for the opponent.

HANSOKU CHUI "Warning" with an IPPON penalty. This is a penalty in which IPPON is added to the opponent's score. HANSOKU-CHUI is usually imposed for infractions for which a KEIKOKU has previously been given in that bout. The Referee points with an index finger to the abdomen of the offender parallel to the floor.

HANTEI "Judgment." Referee calls for judgment by blowing his whistle and the Judges render their decision by flag signal.

HANTEI KACHI "Winner by decision".

HARAI TE Sweeping technique with the arm.

HARAI WAZA Sweeping techniques. In combination, Harai becomes Barai.

HEIAN The Shotokan's name for Kata PINGAN "Peaceful Mind".

HEIKO ZUKI "Parallel Punch" (A double, simultaneous punch).

HEISOKU DACHI An informal attention stance. Feet are together and pointed straight forward.

HENKA WAZA Variations on techniques used after OYO WAZA is applied. HENKA WAZA is varied and many, dependent on the given condition.

HIDARI Left.

HIJI Elbow, also known as Empi.

HIJI-ATE Elbow strike (also called EMPI-UCHI)

HIJI ATEMI Elbow Strikes.

HIJI UKE A blocking action using the elbow.

HIKI-TE The retreating (pulling and twisting) arm during a technique. It gives the balance of power to the forward moving technique. It can also be used as a pulling technique after a grab, or a strike backward with the elbow.

HIKIWAKE "Draw." Referee crosses arms over chest, then uncrosses and holds arms out from the body with the palms showing upwards.

HITOSASHI IPPON KEN Forefinger Knuckle.

HIZA GERI Knee Kick.

HIZA UKE A blocking action using the knee.

HOMBU DŌJŌ A term used to refer to the central dojo of an organization.

HORAN NO KAMAE "Egg in the Nest Ready Position." A "ready" position used in some KATA where the fist in covered by the other hand.

INASU evasion of an on-coming attack through the course of removing the body from the line of attack.

IPPON KEN One Knuckle Fist.

IPPON KUMITE One step sparring.

IPPON NUKITE A stabbing action using the extended index finger.

IPPON SHOBU One point match, used in tournaments.

I.S.O.K. International Society of Okinawan/Japanese Karate-Do.

JIKAN "Time".

JION A kata studied by Green Belts in WKK. The kata is named after the Jion Temple and is one of the longest kata in the WKK system.

JIYU IPPON KUMITE One step free sparring. The participants can attack with any technique whenever ready.

JIYU KUMITE Free Sparring.

JO Wooden staff about 4'-5' in length. The JO originated as a walking stick.

JODAN Upper level. During the practice of KIHON IPPON KUMITE (one step basic sparring), the attacker will normally announce where he/she will attack JODAN, CHUDAN, or GEDAN (Upper level, Midlevel, or Lower level).

JOGAI "Exit from fighting area." The Referee points with his index finger at a 45 degree angle to the area boundary on the side of the offender.

JOGAI KEIKOKU "Second exit from fighting area." WAZA-ARI penalty is given to the opponent.

JOGAI HANSOKU CHUI "Fourth and Final Exit from the fighting area." Fourth exit from the fighting area causes victory to the opponent.

JOGAI HANSOKU CHUI "Third exit from fighting area". Referee uses two hand signals with announcement "AKA (or SHIRO) JOGAI HANSOKU CHUI". He first points with his index finger to the match boundary on the side of the offender, then to the offender's abdomen. An IPPON is awarded to the opponent.

JUJI UKE X Block.

JUN ZUKI The WADO RYU term for OI-ZUKI.

KACHI Victorious. (e.g., AKA KACHI) in a tournament.

KAESU "Turn around".

KAGA DACHI Lady's horse stance.

KAGI ZUKI Hook Punch.

KAISHO Open hand. This refers to the type of blow which is delivered with the open palm. It can also be used to describe other hand blows in which the fist is not fully clenched.

KAKE-TE Hook Block.

KAKIWAKE A two handed block using the outer surface of the wrist to neutralize a two-handed attack, such as a grab.

KAKUSHI WAZA Hidden techniques.

KAKUTO UCHI Wrist joint strike. Also known as "KO UCHI."

KAKUTO UKE Wrist Joint Block. Also known as KO UKE.

KAMAE A posture or stance either with or without a weapon. KAMAE may also connote proper distance (Ma-ai) with respect to one's partner. Although "KAMAE" generally refers to a physical stance, there is an important parallel in Karate between one's physical and one's psychological bearing. Adopting a strong physical stance helps to promote the correlative adoption of a strong psychological attitude. It is important to try so far as possible to maintain a positive and strong mental bearing in Karate.

KAMAE TE A command given by the instructor for students to get into position.

KANKŪ The Shotokan's name for Kata KUSANKU.

KAPPO Techniques of resuscitating people who have succumbed to a shock to the nervous system.

KARATE "Empty Hand". When Karate was first introduced to Japan, it was called "TO-DE", the meaning of TODE is Chinese Hand. The characters of TODE could be pronounced "Karate", and the name was changed to use the characters for Empty Hand.

KARATE-DŌ "The Way of Karate". This implies not only the physical aspect of Karate, but also the mental and spiritual aspects of Karate.

KARATEKA A practitioner of Karate.

KATA A "form" or prescribed pattern of movement. (But also "shoulder.")

KEAGE Snap Kick. (Literally, kick upward).

KEIKO (1) Training. The only secret to success in Karate. (2) Joined Fingertips.

KEIKOKU "Warning with WAZA-ARI penalty in SANBON SHOBU. This is a penalty in which WAZA-ARI is added to the opponent's score. KEIKOKU is imposed for minor infractions for which a warning has previously been given in that bout, or for infractions not sufficiently serious enough to merit HAN-SOKU-CHUI. Referee points an index finger to the feet of the offender at an angle of 45 degrees.

KEKOMI Thrust Kick (Literally, Kick Into/Straight).

KEMPŌ "Fist Law." A generic term to describe fighting systems that uses the fist. In this regard, KARATE is also KEMPO.

KENSEI The technique with silent KIAI. Related to meditation.

KENTSUI Hammer Fist. Also known as TETTSUI.

KENTSUI UCHI (Or TETTSUI UCHI) Hammer Fist Strike.

KERI Kick. In combination, becomes Geri.

KI Mind. Spirit. Energy. Vital-force. Intention. (Chinese "chi") The definitions presented here are very general. KI is one word that cannot be translated directly into any language.

KIAI A shout delivered for the purpose of focusing all of one's energy into a single movement. Even when audible KIAI are absent, one should try to preserve the feeling of KIAI at certain crucial points within Karate techniques. Manifestation of KI (simultaneous union of spirit and expression of physical strength).

KIBA DACHI Straddle Stance. Also known as NAIFANCHI or NAIHANCHI DACHI.

KIHON (Something which is) fundamental. Basic techniques. In WKK, usually called SHINKOKATA.

KIKEN "Renunciation." The Referee points one index finger towards the contestant.

KIME Focus of Power.

KINTEKI Groin. Literally means "Gold Bull's Eye" or "Golden Target".

KI-O-TSUKE "Attention". Musubi Dachi with open hands down both sides.

KIZAMI ZUKI Jab Punch.

KO BO ICHI The concept of "Attack-Defense Connection".

KŌDŌKAN The organization founded by Jigoro Kano where modern Jūdō was developed. This organization had a significant impact on modern Karate.

KŌ EMBUSEN The EMBUSEN, or pattern marked out on the floor, that is shaped like an I. This is the embusen for all for Taikyoku kata..

KO UCHI Wrist joint strike. Also known as KAKUTO UCHI.

KO UKE "Crane Block" or "Arch Block". Same as KAKUTO UKE.

KOHAI Any student junior to you.

KOKEN Wrist Joint.

KOKORO "Spirit, Heart, Mind." In Japanese culture, the spirit dwells in the Heart.

KŌKUTSU DACHI A stance which has most of the weight to the back. Referred to in English as Back Stance.

KOSA DACHI Crossed-Leg Stance.

KOSHIN Rearward.

KOTOWAZA A proverb.

KUATSU The method of resuscitating a person who has lost consciousness due to strangulation or shock.

KUBOTAN A self-defense tool developed by TAKAYUKI KUBOTA. This tool serves normally as a key chain.

KUDANSHA A Black Belt of any degree. Cf. MUDANSHA.

KUMADE Bear hand.

KUMITE Kumite or sparring is a way of practicing Karate techniques with a partner. There are two primary types of kumite: pre-arranged (yakusoku), and free (ju). We focus primarily on yakusoku which is divided into four classifications: basic one-step sparring, three-step sparring, five-step sparring, and semi-free one-step sparring. Although our school does not emphasize sport karate, sparring is an important aspect of our training in the development of technique, attitude, coordination, distance, and judgment.

KUSANKU A pair of kata, Shō and Dai. Kusanku Shō is studied by Brown Belts in WKK, Kusanku Dai by First Degree Black Belts. Named after Koshokun, a famous martial artist. Kusanku and Kanku are variations on the same name, as in fact are Kosokun, Kōshōkun, Kushanku, Kankū, Koushoukun and Kwankū. Kusanku Sho means "Lesser or Little or Minor Kusanku", as opposed to Kusanku Dai, "Greater or Large or Major Kusanku". Despite the names, Kusanku Sho and Dai have about the same number of moves.

KYOSHI "Knowledgeable person," Usually this title is conferred at Rokudan or Shichidan, depending on system. The most common practice in large organizations is for this to be at Shichidan (7th dan).

KYŪ Grade. Any rank below Shodan, i.e. not a Black Belt.

KYUSHO WAZA Pressure point techniques.

MA-AI Proper distancing or timing with respect to one's partner. Since Karate techniques always vary according to circumstances, it is important to understand how differences in initial position affect the timing and application of techniques.

MAAI GA TŌ "Not proper distance"

MAE Front.

MAE EMPI Forward Elbow Strike.

MAE ASHI GERI Kicking with the front leg.

MAE GERI KEAGE Front Snap Kick. Also referred to as MAE KEAGE.

MAE GERI KEKOMI Front Thrust Kick. Also referred to as MAE KEKOMI, or just MAE GERI. This is the kick preferred by Wadō Ki Kai.

MAE UKEMI Forward Fall/Roll.

MAKOTO A feeling of absolute sincerity and total frankness, which requires a pure mind, free from pressure of events.

MANABU Learning by imitating. A method of studying movement and techniques by following and imitating the instructor.

MANJI UKE A double block where one arm executes GEDAN BARAI to one side, while the other arm executes JODAN UCHI UKE (or JODAN SOTO YOKO TE). A manji is a swastika, an ancient Buddhist symbol. The Nazi swastika is a reverse image of the usual Buddhist swastika.

MATSUMURA-SHURI-JION A kata studied by 1st Dan Black Belts in WKK.

MATSUMURA—SHURI-POTSAI A kata studied by 1st Dan Black Belts in WKK.

MATTE "Wait".

MAWASHI GERI Roundhouse Kick.

MAWASHI ZUKI Roundhouse Punch.

MAWASHI EMPI UCHI Circular Elbow Strike. Also referred to as MAWASHI HIJI ATE.

MAWASHI HIJI ATE Circular Elbow Strike. Also referred to as MAWASHI EMPI UCHI.

MAWAT-TE A command given by the instructor for students to turn around. At WKK, "KAESU" is preferred.

MIE NAI "I could not see." A call by a judge to indicate that a given technique was not visible from his/her angle.

MIGI Right, opposite of HIDARI, Left.

MIKAZUKI GERI Crescent Kick.

MOKUSŌ Meditation. Practice often begins or ends with a brief period of meditation. The purpose of meditation is to clear one's mind and to develop cognitive equanimity. Perhaps more importantly, meditation is an opportunity to become aware of conditioned patterns of thought and behavior so that such patterns can be modified, eliminated or more efficiently put to use.

MOROTE ZUKI U-Punch. Punching with both fists simultaneously. Also referred to as AWASE ZUKI.

MOROTE UKE Augmented, or reinforced, Block. One arm and fist support the other arm in a block.

MOTO NO ICHI "Original Position." Contestants, Referee and Judge return to their respective standing lines.

MUDANSHA A karateka who has yet to achieve Black Belt. Cf. KUDANSHA.

MUMOBI "Warning for lack of regard for one's own safety." Referee points one index finger in the air at a 60-degree angle on the side of the offender.

MUMOBI KEIKOKU "Warning with WAZA ARI penalty". Referee uses two hand signals with announcement AKA (SHIRO) MUBOBI-KEIKOKU. He first points with his index finger at a 60 degree angle on the side of the offender, then to the offender's feet.

MUSHIN "No Mind." The state of being that allows freedom and flexibility to react and adapt to a given situation.

MUSUBI DACHI An attention stance with feet pointed slightly outward.

NAGASHI UKE Sweeping Block.

NAGASU "To flow like water". Deflection of an on-coming attack. This term describes being carried by a current in a stream. This relates to nagashi uke in which you re-direct the attack as it moves closer to you, sweeping it just past you.

NAHANCHI A kata studied by Orange Belts in WKK. "Sideway Fighting" or "Back Against the Wall". This kata is also called "Young Plant" as it is the first traditional kata taught in the WKK system. The Shotokan's name for this kata is Tekki. Also spelt or pronounced NAIHANCHI, NAIFUANCHIN, NAIFANCHI, and several other ways.

NAIFANCHI DACHI Straddle Stance. Also referred to as NAIHANCHI DACHI and KIBA DACHI.

NAIHANCHI DACHI Straddle Stance. Also referred to as KIBA DACHI and NAIFANCHI DACHI.

NAKADAKA IPPON KEN Middle Finger Knuckle.

NAMI-GAESHI Returning Wave. Foot technique found in Tekki Shodan to block an attack to the groin area. The technique can also be used to strike the opponent's inner thigh or knee.

NEKO ASHI DACHI Cat Stance.

NIHON NUKITE Two finger stabbing attack.

NIDAN Second Level, as in Second Degree Black Belt.

NIDAN GERI Double Kick.

NIJŪSHIHŌ A kata studied by 1st Dan Black Belts in WKK. "24 Steps".

NISEISHIHŌ Alternate form for NIJUSHIHO. "24 Steps".

NORU "To ride" or "to carry" or "to give a ride to", so you ride on your opponent's attacking arm or leg, etc. You may also ride his HIKITE to break his rhythm; this is very hard to defend.

NUKETE IRU "Out of Target".

NUKITE Spear Hand.

NUNCHAKU An Okinawan weapon consisting of two sticks connected by rope or chain. This was originally used by the Okinawans as a farm tool to thrash rice straw. Also called Numchucks or just Chucks.

OBI A belt.

OI ZUKI Lunge Punch, literally "Chasing Punch".

ONEGAI SHIMASU "I welcome you to train with me," or literally, "I make a request." This is said to one's partner when initiating practice.

OSAE UKE Pressing Block.

OTAGAI NI REI Command to bow to each other as a mark of respect.

OTOSHI EMPI UCHI An elbow strike by dropping the elbow. Also referred to as Otoshi Hiji Ate.

OYAYUBI IPPON KEN Thumb Knuckle.

ŌYŌ WAZA Applications interpreted from techniques in kata, implicated according to a given condition.

PASSAI Alternate transliteration of Kata POTSAI.

PINGAN A series of five kata studied by Yellow and Orange Belts in WKK. Also spelt Pinan, Binan or Pin'an. Pronounced Heian in Modern Standard Japanese. Invented by Yatsusune 'Anko' Itosu (1830-1915). "Peaceful mind".

POTSAI DAI A pair of kata, Shō and Dai. Potsai Dai is studied by Blue Belts in WKK. Also spelt Passai or Bassai. The name means "To Breach a Fortress".

REI "Respect". A method of showing respect in Japanese culture is the Bow. It is proper for the junior person to bow lower than the senior person.

REIGI Etiquette. Also referred to as REISHIKI. Observance of proper etiquette at all times (but especially observance of proper DOJO etiquette) is as much a part of one's training as the practice of techniques. Observation of etiquette indicates one's sincerity, one's willingness to learn, and one's recognition of the rights and interests of others.

REINOJI DACHI A stance with feet making an L-shape.

RENSEI Practice Tournament. Competitors are critiqued on their performances.

RENSHI "A person who has mastered oneself." This person is considered an expert instructor. This status is a prerequisite before attaining the status as KYOSHI. Renshi "has a name." Renshi is no longer one of the many, so to speak. Renshi is usually given at Yodan to Rokudan, depending on the system.

RYŪ Literally "stream", a style or school of Karate.

SAGI ASHI DACHI One Leg Stance. Also referred to as GANKAKU DACHI or TSURU ASHI DACHI.

SAI An Okinawan weapon that is shaped like the Greek letter 'Psi' with the middle being much longer.

SAIFA A kata studied by Green Belts in WKK. The name's meaning is "The Final Breaking Point", or "Destroy & Defeat". Sometimes spelt Saiffa or Saiha.

SANBON KUMITE Three Step Sparring.

SANBON SHOBU Three Point match. Used in tournaments.

SANCHIN DACHI Hour-glass Stance.

SASHITE Raising of the hand either to strike, grab, or block.

SEINCHIN A kata studied by 2nd Dan Black Belts in WKK.

SEIKEN Normal fist, Forefist. Literally "Correct Fist".

SEIRYUTO Bull Strike. A hand technique delivered with the base of the SHUTO (Knife hand).

SEISAN A kata studied in WKK. Also spelt Seishan. One of the advanced Tiger Techniques. The Shotokan's name for this kata is Hangetsu.

SEIZA A proper sitting position. Sitting on one's knees. Sitting this way requires acclimatization, but provides both a stable base and greater ease of movement than sitting cross-legged. It is used for the formal opening and closing of the class.

SEMPAI A senior student.

SEN NO SEN Attacking at the exact moment when the opponent attacks.

SEN SEN NO SEN Attacking before the opponent attacks. Preemptive attack.

SENSEI Teacher. It is usually considered proper to address the instructor during practice as "Sensei" rather than by name. If the instructor is a permanent instructor for one's DŌJŌ or for an organization, it is proper to address the instructor as "Sensei" off the mat as well.

SENSEI NI REI Command to bow to the class Sensei Dojo as a mark of respect.

SHIAI A match or a contest (event).

SHIDOIN Formally recognized Instructor who has not yet be recognized as a SENSEI. Assistant Instructor.

SHIHAN A formal title meaning, approximately, "master instructor." A "teacher of teachers." Hanshi is "wise" or sage-like, hence the common translation of "master." Shinan may be an alternative pronunciation.

SHIKKAKU "Disqualification." This is a disqualification from the actual tournament, competition, or match. The opponent's score is raised to SANBON. In order to define the limit of SHIKKAKU, the Referee Council must be consulted. SHIKKAKU may be invoked when a contestant commits an act which harms the prestige and honor of Karate-Do and when other actions are considered to violate the rules of the tournament. Referee uses two hand signals with the announcement "AKA (SHIRO)—SHIKKAKU." He first points with his index to the offender's face then obliquely above and behind him. The Referee will announce with the appropriate gesture as previously given "AKA (SHIRO) NO KACHI!"

SHIKO DACHI Square Stance. A stance often used in Goju-Ryu and Shito-Ryu.

SHINKOKATA These are the basic techniques which accompany each kata. They consist of blocks, parries, strikes, kicks, punches, etc. which make up the moves of Karate. The longer a student trains, the more complex and demanding the shikokata become.

SHIRO, SHIROI White.

SHIZENTAI Natural Position. The body remains relaxed but alert.

SHOBU HAJIME "Start the Extended Bout".

SHOBU SANBON HAJIME "Start the Bout".

SHŌ Attached to the name of a kata, "Variation". It literally means Little, Lesser, or Minor.

SHŌMEN Front or top of head. Also the designated front of a Dojo.

SHŌMEN NI REI Command to bow to the front of the Dojo as a mark of respect.

SHŌTŌKAN The Japan Karate Association, founded by Gichin Funakoshi.

SHUGO "Judges Called." The Referee beckons with his arms to the Judges.

SHUTO UKE Knife-hand Block.

SOCHIN DACHI Immovable Stance. Also referred to as FUDO DACHI.

SOKUTŌ Edge of foot. This term is often used to refer to the side thrust kick.

SOTO (UDE) UKE Outside (Forearm) Block.

SUKUI UKE Scooping Block.

SUWARI WAZA Techniques from a sitting position.

TACHI Stance.

TAIKYOKO A series of four kata studied by White Belts in WKK.

TAIMING GA OSOI "Not proper timing".

TAI SABAKI Body movement/shifting.

TATE EMPI Upward Elbow Strike.

TATE ZUKI Vertical Punch. A fist punch with the palm along a vertical plane.

TATE URAKEN UCHI Vertical back-fist attack.

TEIJI DACHI A stance with the feet in a 'T-shape.'

TEI EMBUSEN A EMBUSEN with the floor pattern in a 'T-shape.'

TEISHŌ UCHI Palm Heel Strike.

TEISHŌ UKE Palm Heel Block.

TEKKI The Shotokan name for Kata NAHANCHI.

TETTSUI UCHI Hammer Strike. Also called KENTSUI.

TOBI GERI Jump Kick.

TONFA A farm tool developed into a weapon by the Okinawans.

TORANAI "No Point"

TORIMASEN "Unacceptable as scoring techniques." As HIKIWAKE, but culminating with the palms facing downwards towards body.

TSUKAMI WAZA Catching technique. A blocking technique by seizing the opponent's weapon, arm, or leg. Used often for grappling techniques.

TSUKI A punch. Literally thrust. In combination, becomes Zuki or Dzuki.

TSURU ASHI DACHI Crane Stance, also referred to as GANKAKU DACHI and SAGI ASHI DACHI.

TSUZUKETE "Fight On!" Resumption of fighting ordered when unauthorized interruption occurs.

TSUZUKETE HAJIME "Resume Fighting—Begin!" Referee standing upon his line, steps back into ZENKUTSU DACHI and brings the palms of this hands toward each other.

TUITE Grappling skills.

UCHI Strike.

UCHI DESHI A live-in student. A student who lives in a dojo and devotes him/herself both to training and to the maintenance of the dojo (and sometimes to personal service to the SENSEI of the dojo).

UCHI MAWASHI GERI Inside Roundhouse Kick.

UCHI (UDE) UKE Inside (Forearm) Block.

UKE Block. Literally "Receive".

UKEMI WAZA Breakfall techniques.

UNSA A kata studied by Purple Belts in WKK. Hand in the Clouds or Clouds Hands.

UNSU A kata studied by 2nd Dan Black Belts in WKK.

URA ZUKI An upper cut punch used at close range.

URAKEN Back Knuckle.

USEISHI A kata studied by 2nd Dan Black Belts in WKK.

USHIRO EMPI UCHI Striking to the rear with the elbow.

USHIRO GERI Back Kick.

WADŌ KI KAI A style of Karate headed by Arce Sensei.

WANSHŪ An old name for Kata EMPI.

WAZA Technique(s).

WAZA ARI "Half point"

WKK WADŌ KI KAI.

YAMA ZUKI Mountain Punch. A wide U-shaped dual punch.

YAME Stop!

YASUMI Rest. A term used by the instructor to have the students relax, normally following a long series of drills.

YŌI Ready.

YOKO Side.

YOKO GERI KEAGE Side Snap Kick. Also referred to as YOKO KEAGE.

YOKO GERI KEKOMI Side Thrust Kick. Also referred to as YOKO KEKOMI.

YOKO MAWASHI EMPI UCHI Striking with the elbow to the side.

YOKO TOBI GERI Flying Side Kick.

YOWAI "Weak Focus"

YUDANSHA Black Belt holder (any dan).

ZANSHIN Lit. "Remaining mind/heart." Even after a Karate technique has been completed, one should remain in a balanced and aware state. ZANSHIN thus connotes "following through" in a technique, as well as preservation of one's awareness so that one is prepared to respond to additional attacks.

ZA-REI The traditional Japanese bow from the kneeling position.

ZENKUTSU DACHI Front Stance, Forward Stance.

ZENSHIN Forward.

ZORI Japanese slippers. Flip-flops.

ZUKI Combining form of Tsuki, Punch.

Index

0-595-30747-7

Printed in the United States
28730LVS00003B/181

9 780595 307470